12 Essential Laws
for Becoming Indispensable

by
Dr. Tony Zeiss

Published by Executive Books
206 West Allen Street
Mechanicsburg, PA 17055
Telephone: 800-233-2665
Fax: 717-766-6565
www.executivebooks.com
www.tremendousjones.com

Printed in the United States of America

ISBN: 0-937539-36-8
LCCN: 99-61671

Contents

Foreword

By
Zig Ziglar

The laws presented in Tony Zeiss's book reflect the positive principles I've promoted all my life. It is no surprise that American employers value positive attitudes, effective communication skills, integrity, good work ethic, teamwork, and technical know how. It's these human qualities that have always separated the successful from the unsuccessful, the happy from the unhappy, and the healthy from those who are unhealthy.

Dr. Zeiss has captured the essence of what it takes to build successful careers, but even more that that, his 12 laws for becoming indispensable offer a prescription for living quality lives. Academic and skills training is essential for career success these days, but learning effective workplace and social skills is equally important. Unfortunately, these social-behavioral skills are seldom taught in our schools and colleges. This research-based book was designed to fill that void and to equip you with a clear understanding and ability to demonstrate those essential skills employers value today.

This easy-to-read book is written in a clear and crisp manner, filled with practical examples and useful skill assessments. The genius of the work, however, is that the book exhibits the collective wisdom of over a score of successful business and corporate CEO's. The advice from these admired professionals elevates the value of this book far beyond its basic research and good advice.

My advice to anyone who wants to be successful in the work environment is to read this book! My advice to any employer who desires a highly productive, energized, and effective workforce team is to give this book to each and every employee.

Preface

You can achieve these twelve essential laws for becoming indispensable! The sooner you learn them and use them, the sooner you will find the career success you seek. Using these laws at work will help you in job advancements and will provide the best job security possible. But first, a word of warning. You will not be successful using these laws to keep or advance in a job unless you are prepared to take them and use them seriously and consistently.

Most underemployed or unemployed workers feel rejected, defeated, cheated, or perplexed. They usually go through an emotional process similar to the stages of grief, that is, denial, followed by anger, depression, fear, sometimes guilt, and finally acceptance. These changing emotions are quite normal. Unfortunately, emotions and innermost feelings drive beliefs and shape self-concept. In consequence, what you feel, you believe. And belief drives behavior. If you are depressed or angry when you have an interview for a promotion or when you network for advancement opportunities, your speech, your posture, and all of your nonverbal actions telegraph that depression or anger. That is why you have to work through any negative feelings surrounding your current employment condition and get on with the positive and successful adventure of moving toward complete career success. Strap on your seat belt, you are already on your way toward becoming indispensable!

You can use scores of resources to become indispensable and advance in your career. But, your network of friends inside and outside the company or organization you work for will be your best resource. Libraries, community colleges, and small business development centers can help you learn some techniques for increasing your value to your employer. But it is up to you—and only you—to sell yourself. In this respect, it's your relationship with others and their perception of your value at the workplace that really matters. The twelve essential laws presented in this book will guide you in selling yourself successfully to any peer group, supervisor, or employer.

You can use any number of gimmicks to give yourself an edge in the job-security, job-advancement process. Using your unique charm, being in all the right places at the right times, and always agreeing with your supervisors can help, but using the twelve laws described in this book will be significantly more effective. Ignore any of them and all the flattery and gimmicks in the world will not help. Each law is unique. Learn them, live them, and use them to your advantage.

These twelve laws present the primary traits employers want in employees. The top ten laws are mostly attitudinal in nature. That is, you can make them a part of your life by believing in them and deciding to use them. You see, positive behavior is essential to career success. The remaining two laws emphasize work preparation and prior experience.

The formula for a secure and successful career is this: (1) believe in yourself, (2) focus on your career goal, and (3) employ the twelve essential laws for becoming indispensable!

Acknowledgments

Many thanks to my wife, Beth, to Zig Ziglar, to Wendy Stone, and to the people who helped in the reviewing of this book:

Ron and Katherine Harper
Harper Corporation of America
Bill Dowdell, President
American Flexographic Association
Bob Hanley
General Motors Corporation

Introduction

Can one really become "indispensable" at the workplace? Not so much in the literal sense because we have emerged into a knowledge-based and global economy where change is constant and no one can completely control the variable dimensions of his or her employment. However, everyone can significantly enhance his or her job security and career advancement opportunities by consistently exhibiting those skills and behaviors supervisors and employers most admire. These same skills and behaviors will help you with job acquisition success if you are ever separated from a job. You may not be totally indispensable in a specific work setting, but you can become indispensable in the broader marketplace.

Unfortunately, most workers do not realize that they have almost unlimited control over their careers and work conditions. Some workers, for instance, develop the misconception that they are inadequate, under skilled, or discriminated against because of age, race, gender, size, or any number of self-created excuses to protect their fragile egos. This is typical, but self-defeating, behavior. Regardless of your situation, you can and must emphasize your strengths and have the confidence to sell yourself to your supervisors and employer.

As the United States shifts into a global economy, its businesses are moving into a perpetual state of rightsizing. That is, they downsize to become more competitive and upsize as demands for their new products and services increase. Corporate America, and in some cases the public sector, is reengineering to increase its competitive stature by focusing on more efficient processes, greater productivity, and reduced labor costs. In short, America's private and public employers are undergoing a continuous process of job elimination and job creation as a necessary competitive technique. This is a natural process. Consider jobs in agriculture. In 1900, 5 percent of the workforce was in agriculture. Today, less than 2 percent of the workforce is employed in this area. The average worker today will change jobs seven times and change careers three times during his or her working years. Sure, 42 million American jobs have been lost since 1980, but 71 million new jobs have been created during the same seventeen or eighteen year period. Opportunities to reach career success have never been better!

Smart American workers have become entrepreneurial and view themselves as enterprises, commodities to be marketed at the workplace. The good news is that most of today's employers are desperate to find and keep productive workers. Our national unemployment rate has been at or below five percent for several years and the work climate is very good for all who are willing to be productive and enthusiastic.

To survive in this new work environment, you must understand how to best prepare yourself and sell yourself in the job market and at the workplace. You can do this by developing a clear career goal, getting the necessary skills, and by undertaking and practicing the traits employers most seek in their employees. Successful career professionals know how to leave the past behind them and look ever forward to their goal. They know that the best predictor of success is to have a clear goal, a positive expectation to achieve it, and the self-discipline to continuously work toward it.

America has entered the age of the knowledge worker. The demand for knowledge-based skills is essential for anyone who aspires to become indispensable and successful in a career. Company presidents are telling me that credentials are still important, but the ability to transform knowledge into performance is the critical factor that determines an employee's value. Truett Cathy, founder and CEO of Chick Fil-A restaurants, recently visited the college I am privileged to lead. While on a campus tour, he addressed two classes of culinary students and offered this advice. "Academic credentials are important and will help you get in the door, but performance and dependability will get you success." Once a career goal has been established, the ability to access information, process information, and apply information at the workplace becomes a critical component of successful workers. In the end, your best opportunity to reach your career goal and become indispensable depends almost entirely upon you and your reputation at work.

After thirty years of helping people with job training, job acquisition, and career advancement skills, I have fleshed out the twelve attributes that employers most prefer among potential and existing employees. As a state job training council chair, college president, and chair of the National Workforce Development

Commission and Chairman of the Board for the American Association of Community Colleges, I can attest that these twelve personal traits make all the difference between successful and unsuccessful careers.

I call these job acquisition/retention attributes the twelve essential laws for becoming indispensable. You will dramatically increase your chances for success by learning and using these laws in your efforts to retain or advance in a job.

Chapter 1
Double A's

ENTHUSIASM IS CONTAGIOUS!

THE FIRST AND MOST IMPORTANT LAW
FOR BECOMING INDISPENSABLE IS HAVING
ALTITUDE IN YOUR ATTITUDE!

The most important attribute for becoming indispensable is a positive attitude. And guess who has absolute control over your attitude? You are correct! You alone determine how you will face each day, react to each circumstance, and behave toward others. People, especially employers, want to be associated with positive, can do people, happy people.

You can verify the truth of this successful job-seeking trait by answering these questions:

- Do I enjoy working with positive or negative people?

- Who most often gets promotions, negative or positive people?

- Do positive or negative people most often reach their career goals?

The answers are obvious. Optimistic, cheerful people are fun to be around and usually do well in their careers.

Employer research indicates that a positive attitude is nearly always at the very top of the list of desirable characteristics for employees. Further, employees who are happy in their careers are most likely to be identified as "rising stars" by management. It's no wonder, then, that the most successful people have positive attitudes.

I can cite scores of examples of people who lost positions or failed to get promotions because of their poor attitudes. These people seem to relish their chronic discontent, and then complain when employers dismiss them or refuse to promote them. Unfortunately, it is easy to get caught up with the whiners and complainers. Misery likes company and these folks will befriend anyone who joins in with and reinforces their negative beliefs. We humans become what we think about all day long and in a short time we can become negative about everything without realizing it. Each time we are passed over for a raise or new assignment, our negative attitude is reinforced and our viewpoint is reconfirmed. By seeking the sympathy of others, our viewpoint is hardened into anger or a perpetual pity party. Some experts believe negative thinking is addictive. Fortunately, this destructive way of thinking that can be broken by simply changing one's attitude. Changing peer groups at work can also be very healthy.

By determining to become happy, enthusiastic, and optimistic, we will soon become happy, enthusiastic, and optimistic. By thinking and speaking negatively we become negative. By thinking and speaking positively, we become positive. The choice is entirely up to each of us to determine what kind of person we wish to become.

Anxiety as an Ally

A major key to a successful career is to develop and maintain a success-oriented attitude from the very beginning. Overcoming self-doubt, anger, bitterness, and other self-defeating attitudes is often the greatest challenge for workers in transition. As John Belk of Belk Department Stores often advises, "Whining about your problems to others is a waste of time; half of them don't care and the other half are glad you've got them." This is an overstatement, of course, but the point is well made. Each of us must resolve to be either a whiner or a winner.

Whether you are involved in trying to keep your position or getting a promotion, you have reason to feel some anxiety. But you can leverage the anxiety into a powerful ally to be successful. You see a little anxiety keeps you mentally alert and drives you into action. Even if the worst happens and you get caught in a downsizing, do not panic. You would not be alone out there in the job-seeking market. The U.S. Department of Labor reports that 5.7 percent of the employment population or nearly fourteen million workers are in transition today in these United States! You see, people are changing jobs as employment demands change and as they pursue their career goals. The good news is that we're in the middle of an expanding economy, and millions of new jobs are being created every decade in our great country. The better news is that virtually all fourteen million of America's transitional workers will find a good job if they keep a positive attitude, gain the appropriate skills, and remain persistent. As a matter of fact, U.S. government statistics indicate that approximately 22 percent of American workers, nearly 30 million people, find new employment each year. This means 2.5 million people find new employment each month, 625,000 each week, and 125,000 each day. With the proper attitude, the odds of getting new employment are very good. Remember, you are not unemployed; you're simply a worker in transition as everyone is at some time in life.

But life's been unfair to me, you may be thinking. Welcome to the club! Life is full of unfairness, unhappiness, and negativism. We can clamor all we want about the unfairness of life's circumstances, but absolutely nothing will change the circumstances unless we resolve to change them through conscious action. At this point in your life you may not feel in control. But you'll always have the option to be in control of one thing—your attitude. You see, it's not what happens *to* you that matters; it's what happens *in* you that matters. By controlling your attitude, in a certain sense you control your destiny.

Working in an atmosphere of low morale is always difficult. Unfortunately, too many people choose to believe their morale is determined by their supervisors or by the actions of others. In truth, people should not allow their morale to be determined by anyone except themselves. Mature, successful people choose to be responsible for their morale, regardless of their circumstances.

Facing the Day

Only one person can decide how you will face each day. The temptation to seek safety, to avoid taking risks, to give up on dreams is forever around you. But positive people know how to keep faith in themselves and in their abilities. You can control your thoughts, and your thoughts control your emotions and attitudes. If you don't like the facts, you can change your attitudes about them. It takes some practice, but millions of people do it every day. By looking at any situation from a detached viewpoint, you can begin to see different, even positive, dimensions of the situation. How many times have you worried yourself sick over something that never materialized? Or more likely, how many times have you experienced something terribly negative in your life only to see it as a positive growth experience in retrospect?

One technique that often helps to reduce excess anxiety or worry is to ask yourself the following questions when you are faced with a major problem:

- Does it threaten my soul?

- Does it threaten my family?

- Does it threaten my life?

- How important will this be fifty or one hundred years from now?

This exercise helps you get in control of your thoughts about your transitional or anxiety-producing employment condition by developing the proper perspective. Once you can control your thoughts, you can eliminate negative thinking and replace it with a positive, success-oriented attitude. You become positive simply by thinking positively!

Advice from the Pros

Successful people are noted for their persistent optimism and infectious cheerfulness. They are fun to be around because they are so encouraging. Is it any wonder that supervisors and employers also prefer to have positive employees?

In preparation for this book, I surveyed some of America's most prominent employers and some not so well known. These employers are representative of a variety of business types, sizes, and geographic locations in order to verify a consistent and comprehensive assessment of what it takes to become indispensable. Appendix A provides a collection of specific characteristics, skills, and behaviors these employers most value in their workers. A review of them should be revealing and helpful as you determine to move up in your career by becoming indispensable. For this chapter, I surveyed three friends of mine, all of whom are extremely successful in their careers and learned how to become invaluable in their own right.

Zig Ziglar, a famous motivational speaker and writer regularly participates in national speaking tours with notables like President George Bush and Barbara Bush, Colen Powell, Dr. Robert Schuller and others. He has written several best seller books focused on helping people achieve their dreams, and is chairman of the board of Ziglar Training Systems.

Zig has this to say about the importance of a good attitude: "Having a good attitude is extremely important for peak performing employees. With the right attitude you will acquire the other skills necessary for success."

Zig's advice to people who want to advance and become invaluable employees is: "Develop and use the qualities of integrity, dependability, optimism, competence, enthusiasm, commitment, hard work, and teamwork. Also, share your knowledge and enthusiasm to help others grow. Those who move ahead do so because they develop and teach others."

John Belk, Chairman of the Board for Belks, Inc. which operates over 250 department stores throughout the Southeast, also had a successful political career, serving as the mayor of Charlotte, North Carolina. Business and political leaders from across the country seek Mr. Belk's expertise and advice. His corporation employs 27,000 people.

John has this to say about the importance of a good attitude: "With a can do, optimistic attitude you can accomplish almost anything. With a collection of employees who have this same positive attitude, your

company can accomplish almost anything and overcome nearly every adversity. Positive attitudes are
essential for employees who aspire to become indispensable."

John's advice to people who want to advance and
become invaluable employees is: "Be loyal to your
employer and to your supervisor, but mostly to your
customers. Demonstrate how your work contributes to
the economic health of the company and you won't have
to worry about job security."

Jim Bavis, Vice President of Employee Relations for
Sprint, is an accomplished attorney, a distinguished
graduate of the Institute of Labor and Industrial
Relations, University of Illinois, and is nationally
known for his expertise in labor relations litigation and
human resources management. Sprint employs 50
thousand people.

Jim has this to say about the importance of a good
attitude: "Each action taken at the workplace eventually translates into a negative or a positive experience
by the customer. Positive people generally produce positive customer experiences and negative people generally produce negative customer contacts. Companies
and organizations live and die according to their relationship with customers. Positive employees are essential for company success."

Jim's advice to people who want to advance and
become invaluable employees is: "Resolve to be the
most positive and enthusiastic employee in your divi-

sion or department. Strive to be the model for developing customer loyalty and you will be valued greatly."

The point is obvious. If you want to be successful at becoming indispensable and having a rewarding, successful career, be positive and project enthusiasm!

Conclusion

People with successful careers almost always have a clear career goal in mind, they have faith in themselves, and they jump into the career advancement process with relish. They make up their minds to view their work as an adventure, and they see themselves as a desirable product or service to be marketed. Most of all, they have an unquenchable spirit of optimism and cheerfulness, and they know that the impressions they make on others are important, especially the first one. A constant review of the altitude of the attitude is essential for all successful workers. This law of attitude will contribute to your career success and happiness more than any other law reviewed in this book.

Practical Advice

Remember that employers value and promote employees with good, can do attitudes. Make up your mind right now to concentrate on your blessings and your strengths, not your troubles. Make a conscious decision to be cheerful and optimistic. As Vince Lombardi used to say, "If you're not fired with enthusiasm, you'll be fired with enthusiasm." Demonstrate your positive attitude by practicing it in every situation and in everything you do. Try to focus all of your attention on the person or persons with whom you're talking. You especially need to be positive during all direct contacts with anyone who can potentially help you keep or advance in your career.

You must learn to control your attitude by thinking positively in all situations and at all times so that you, in fact, become positive. The first few seconds of all job promotion interviews are most important. Your broad smile, confident posture, firm handshake, and sincere greeting are essential in making a good impression. I've interviewed thousands of people and assisted thousands more who sought employment, and I can tell you unequivocally that my impression of them was always determined within the first minute or so of our meeting each other. Yes, sometimes that initial impression changed over time, but first impressions die hard, and most job or job promotion seekers never get a second chance to change that impression. Frankly, if I don't see excitement in the eye, cheerfulness in the heart, and a genuine positive nature within the applicant, I move to the next finalist. The lesson? Make that first impression a great one by having an uplifting, enthusiastic, and consistently positive attitude!

Points to Ponder

1. Resolve to be happy.
2. Stay positive.
3. Career success is attainable.
4. Keep the faith.
5. Make work an adventure.
6. Impressions are lasting.

From This Day Forward

(This section, which will appear at the end of each chapter, is designed to help you internalize and apply each law in your daily life.)

1. Example: "I will be cheerful, enthusiastic, and grateful for my blessings."

2. Example: "I will not participate in whining, criticizing, or demeaning others."

3. Example: "I will view my work as an adventure!"

4. _____.

Part Two: The Way Forward

Chapter 2
The Capital C

COMMUNICATE WELL OR BE FOREVER MISUNDERSTOOD!

THE SECOND MOST IMPORTANT LAW FOR BECOMING INDISPENSABLE IS BEING AN EFFECTIVE COMMUNICATOR!

Many people think that technical skills and prior experience are the most important determinants for becoming indispensable in today's sophisticated workplace. They are wrong. Survey after survey of America's employers indicates that the most successful employees are those who can communicate well. In fact, my research indicates that the possession of specific technical skills and prior experience rank as the lowest two laws for getting a job. Of course, they are absolutely necessary for career success, but there are ten laws before them that are critical for becoming indispensable.

All the knowledge and technical skills known to humanity are useless to an employer unless you can communicate to other people. If you have good technical skills and experience in a career field, but you have problems getting, keeping, or advancing in a job, the chances are high that you have violated the second law of becoming indispensable.

The capital C law underscores the critical dimension of communication. People judge us in large measure by the way we communicate. Unfair as it may sound, the truth is, people evaluate us by the way they see and hear us. Everyone communicates, but not everyone communicates effectively. The law of communicating to become indispensable emphasizes the need to (1) make a good impression, (2) project confidence, and (3) build trusting relationships quickly. People who become effective at using the law of communication in this respect will have few problems advancing and remaining employed in their chosen career field.

You can demonstrate the truth of this law by answering the following questions:

- How many really good communicators have I known who were out of work very long?

- If I had my choice to spend a social evening with a good communicator or a poor communicator, which one would I select?

- If an employer has the choice (and he or she usually has) of promoting a good communicator or a poor one, which applicant do I think will get the promotion?

The ability to make effective group presentations is becoming increasingly important to career success, but this law of communication mostly involves basic interpersonal communication skills. Managers consistently rate verbal skills, nonverbal skills, and writing skills as key skills of those considered for promotions. I have interviewed hundreds of applicants for jobs and promotions who have had impeccable credentials and impressive resumes, but their interviews, body language, and/or cover letters cost them any chance of serious consideration. I have also been in the uncomfortable position of having to determine who remains employed and who is to be released because of market conditions. With the knowledge base being equal, those with the best attitudes and best communication skills kept their employment. One more thing, if you really want to move up in your career, make sure you tell your supervisors about your goal. They will respect you for having set a career vision and you will be on their mind when promotions and new assignments become available.

The Supervisor

Just put yourself in the place of your supervisor for a moment. As the person making decisions about who remains with the organization or gets the next promotion, your credibility and judgment are on the line. Your next promotion may well depend on your ability to identify the most productive people. If you are the owner of a company, your ability to search out the best employees among many becomes even more essential. The very existence of your business may depend on it.

Now let's assume you are screening all employees in your work unit for a possible promotion and must narrow them to three finalists to be interviewed. Chances are good that you will first measure the applicants' minimum qualifications for the position. Beyond that, your knowledge of each individual at the workplace will heavily influence your decision making process. You will mentally review your personal association with each employee, particularly in respect to their ability to work with others, contribute to the productivity of the organization, and their attitude in general. It is no coincidence that each of these skill sets requires good interpersonal communication skills.

Pretend you have selected your three finalists and have set up interviews. The primary purpose of the interview is to help you promote the best person for the position. This is your opportunity to meet the candidates face-to-face. If you do not know the finalists well, ninety-nine times out of one hundred you will promote the finalist who makes the best impression during the interview. The interviewee who speaks with the most confidence, who listens best, and who has the best overall appearance and body language is the one you will promote. If you know and have confidence in the interviewees, it is a safe bet that you will promote the employee with whom you communicate best or feel the most rapport. You will also promote those who have been the most productive, are committed to the organization, and are loyal. In short, employers and supervisors are just like you. Once all things are mostly equal, they will hire the person they feel best about, the person they are impressed with the most. In every employment situation the objective process of checking qualifications, experience, and references eventually shifts to a subjective process of intuition, feeling, and general impressions. The applicant who has the best attitude and communication skills inevitably gets the promotion.

Most employers clearly understand that people make or break their businesses. This recognition has caused employers to become experts at human resources management. Some of them use a sophisticated system for selecting and retaining employees while others simply review applications and resumes. In either case, however, the gut feeling they get from the interview or from prior association with the applicant really drives their decision to keep, release, or promote individuals. *But that's just not fair,* you might be thinking. Fair or not, when it's your career or your business that's at stake, the survival instinct is very strong, and interviewers, within the parameters of the law, will choose the person they think to be best for the position. The good news is that you can take advantage of the capital C law by learning to be a great communicator.

ADVICE FROM THE PROS

Building trusting relationships is the secret of successful people the world over. This is especially true at the workplace where communication, teamwork, and trust are so critical. Three nationally respected business leaders offer the following advice regarding the importance of interpersonal communication at the workplace.

Rolfe Neill, former publisher of the Charlotte Observer, an award winning Knight Ridder newspaper with a daily circulation of 240 thousand, views the ability to communicate as a critical human characteristic.

Rolfe had this to say about the importance of communication skills for peak performing employees: "Communications is the heart of all human relations and human relations is at the heart of all human activity. Therefore, good communication skills are paramount-whether you're a janitor or a chairman."

Rolfe's advice to people who want to advance and become invaluable employees is: "Take any job given to you, do it better than anyone else, then ask for more."

Billy Ray, President of Bell South for North Carolina, and a renowned negotiator in federal telecommunications regulations, understands the importance of being able to communicate clearly.

Billy says this about the importance of communicating well:

"Excellent communication skills are a must. These include: listening, leading by example, giving clear directions and expectations, inspiring confidence and motivating others. Good communication does not necessarily require a great vocabulary or excellent writing skills, but it does require the ability to connect with other people."

Billy's advice to people who want to advance and become invaluable employees is: "Be involved, be responsible, be a team player, and step forward to do the job with integrity and character."

William J. Ryan is Senior Vice President of Human Resources for Sea-Land Service, Incorporated, an international company that moves goods throughout the world in bulk containers on ships, railcars, airplanes, and trucks. This remarkable company operates in over 80 countries and employs approximately nine thousand people.

Bill says: "Effective communication is the cornerstone for effective leadership. It is the competency that is essential to be a leader at the workplace."

Bill has this advice for people who wish to become indispensable at the workplace: "Get involved and understand the global market and your business. Make things happen, take risks, and build friendships at work."

Finally, Mark Ethridge, CEO for a multi-state publishing organization which produces weekly business journals has this input. "Having good communication skills is vital at the workplace. It's not possible to be a peak performer without being a great communicator. What good is an idea if it can't be effectively shared?"

His advice to people who want to advance and become invaluable is straightforward: "Do more than is expected of you."

The secret to becoming indispensable, according to some of America's most respected employers, is to learn to communicate well, be knowledgeable in your job, and be more productive than everyone else in your work area.

Assess Yourself

You will do well to assess your communication strengths and weaknesses then conscientiously work to improve. Often, your best friend or your spouse will be honest enough to point them out to you. In any event, attending a class or seminar on communication techniques is advisable. Brushing up on communication skills is always a good idea since these skills generally assist in all of life's endeavors. An assessment of your adeptness in the following areas will be most useful for becoming indispensable:

- Speech. Seek an honest critique of your ability to speak in casual and in formal settings. Employers especially value your skills at making presentations. Your peers value your interpersonal, conversational skills. Good telephone skills and etiquette are essential. Be sure your volume and intonation are adequate and your diction is good. Work at eliminating anything that distracts from your effectiveness when speaking.

- Body language. Believe it or not, your body language speaks volumes to the observer. Assess your posture in a variety of settings. Photographs and videotape recordings are especially revealing. Concentrate on holding eye contact, keeping pleasant facial expressions, and remaining poised in all circumstances.

- Writing. Get someone to review your writing skills, particularly as they apply to memorandums, reports, E-mail, and thank-you notes. Grammar checks and spell checks are nice on the computer, but they are no substitute for effective writing.

- Communication etiquette. Seek an honest assessment of your ability to listen well and to participate in social conversations. Do you encourage conversation by introducing topics and by asking questions of others? Do you stay focused on other people's thoughts or are your own more interesting to you?

- Paralanguage. The best conversationalist is an active listener. Does your paralanguage—verbal sounds of agreement, surprise, understanding, and disagreement, for example—encourage and compliment others when they're talking?

Many of these communication attributes come naturally to you. Others are not so natural, but you can learn them. However you choose to learn to communicate effectively, you must be able to gain people's confidence through sincerity. One technique for developing good communication skills is to emulate someone whom you think does well in this area. It could be a politician, a teacher, a salesperson, or anyone who has proven success in dealing with others on a consistent basis. Confidence comes from being prepared. After you have brushed up on your communication skills, anticipate every question regarding career promotion interviews. (See chapter 9 for a sample list of interview questions.) After a short time, your answers will be spontaneous, and your sincerity will show.

If you have a serious communication deficiency, do not lose heart. Helen Keller could neither speak, hear, nor talk yet she was graduated from Radcliffe and became an internationally famous author and lecturer. Consider Moses of Old Testament times. His brother Aaron often spoke for him in formal settings because Moses had a speech affliction. Yet Moses became one of the most important figures in his time or anyone else's.

Conclusion

Communicating effectively is an essential law for becoming indispensable. It begins with planning and ends with making a great impression on paper, electronically, and during day to day communication with others. Once you have chosen the career path and career goal you most wish to get, plan for it and develop the confidence that you will be the best among your peers.

Making a good impression seldom happens by accident. The secret to making a good impression is to become a good communicator. Listen to others as intently as you would listen to a toddler's first words. Be friendly, contribute to conversations, and always keep a sense of humor. Your subordinates, peers, and superiors at the workplace will come to respect and appreciate you. Manager's value good communicators, people with visions, and people who are loyal to them and the organization. Just be sincere and be yourself—your best self—and you will increase your chances for promotions and for progressing in your career. Strive to become a good communicator and you'll be astonished at how easy it is to make a good impression, project confidence, and build trusting relationships.

Practical Advice

Remember that employers and managers behave just as you would if you were in their place. Employers and managers look for the best candidate for each available position and would much rather promote a known employee than to recruit someone unknown to them. They do this through an objective screening process and through a subjective, impression-based process. Your attitude is extremely important, but your ability to communicate is also important. Make a conscious decision to assess your verbal and nonverbal communication skills, and resolve to improve by adopting techniques of successful people and by attending a communication class or seminar. Answering anticipated questions with sincerity and thought is essential during networking as well as during promotional interviews. But you must not overlook making a good impression through facial expressions, posture, and listening skills. The lesson? Be prepared, be sincere, and communicate with confidence!

Points to Ponder

1. Learn to communicate well.

2. Project confidence.

3. Build trusting relationships.

4. Make good impressions continuously.

5. Evaluate strengths and weaknesses in communication.

6. Get the training you need.

From This Day Forward

1. I will communicate better by listening more and concentrating on the other person's problems and ideas.

2. _____.

3. _____.

4. _____.

Chapter 3
Think 110 Percent

WORK WORTH DOING IS WORTH DOING WELL.

THE THIRD LAW FOR BECOMING
INDISPENSABLE IS HAVING A
STRONG WORK ETHIC!

"**J**ust send me someone who will come to work drug-free, on time, and with a good attitude and they'll have a good career with us!" As president of a large community college, I hear this same appeal from employers practically every day. As I speak around the country about workforce development, the story is the same. Employers value productive employees, people with good work ethic. Employees who show up on time, are productive, and enjoy going that extra mile inevitably have high job security and get promoted over those who show no enthusiasm or dedication to the company or their careers.

American companies are in the wealth creation business. They create products or provide services that generate a profit. This profit is inevitably spread into the economy as the company pays its employees, pays taxes, distributes dividends to its stockholders, and spends money on new equipment and new employees for expansion. People, lots of them, benefit from these wealth creation enterprises. In many respects, people and companies are pursuing the same goal – to better their condition through the acquisition of wealth. Smart workers understand that loyalty and high productivity will help them better achieve their own goals for wealth and a better condition. Smart employers, (and most of them are), value committed and productive employees who care about the company. This, in its simplified form, is referred to as good work ethic. Appendix A features a detailed list of work ethic descriptions. Through our system of free enterprise, America has had more than two hundred years to encourage a strong work ethic, and that is precisely what employers have come to expect.

You can verify the truth of this important law by answering the following questions:

- If I am paying someone to paint my house, do I want the painter to do a quick job, a mediocre job, or a thoroughly professional job including cleanup?

- If I'm paying someone by the hour to repair my automobile, how often would I want him to take breaks or chat with coworkers?

- When I've employed someone to repair my plumbing, do I expect it to be halfway, mostly, or totally fixed?

Your answers are the same as everyone else's. We expect to get our money's worth from people we pay to render a service. Companies and corporations deserve the same from their employees. After all, businesses are owned and operated by people just like the rest of us. I have participated in the recruitment for scores of companies that were expanding or relocating their businesses, and the work ethic of available employees is always a top concern. In fact, the ability to get and keep well-trained employees with strong work ethics is the number one incentive for new, expanding, or relocating businesses. American businessmen and businesswomen recognize that people make their company successful or unsuccessful, and that is why training and work ethic are so important to them. The only way businesses can survive in the global marketplace is to out produce or give better service than their competitors. And the only way they can out perform their competitors is through the use of excellent employees, professionals who are willing to give 110 percent all the time. Loyalty is also an essential attribute of good work ethics. The following advice, written by Elbert Hubbard in "Get Out or Get in Line," Selected Writing of Elbert Hubbard, PP. 59-60 (1928) is as solid today as it was seventy years ago:

"If you work for a man, in heaven's name work for him! If he pays you wages that supply you your bread and butter, work for him-speak well of him, think well of him, stand by him and stand by the institution he represents If put to the pinch, an ounce of loyalty is worth a pound of cleverness."

The Profit Factor

In a free market economy, your ability to compete in the marketplace determines whether you make a profit or lose your shirt. Employers understand this fundamental principle, and they are interested in employees who also understand it. Private employers look for employees who understand that *profit* is not a dirty word and that job security is directly tied to their productivity. As cruel as it sounds, no one owes anyone else a job, job security, or job advancement. Further, no one should feel entitled to promotions or salary increases unless their productivity and worth to the organization increases. You have to earn your position by preparing for it and you will keep your position by helping the employer make a profit. In short, your ability to outproduce your competition ultimately determines your success on the job or in a career.

In today's global economy, we can depend on one common truth: If a society wants to live well, it must produce well. I would take this truth one step farther and state if you want to live well, you must produce well. You see, people and their ability to out produce their competitors really drive the economy. Government does not drive the economy, and neither do corporations; people drive it. Subsequently, individual productivity is directly related to individual economic success, just as the collective productivity of a company is directly related to the company's economic success.

It is natural for us to want the highest salary we can get, to be appreciated for our work, and to be a part of something important. Most American employers are willing to provide these job satisfactions if we are willing to contribute our best toward making the business successful. I recently visited with John Correnti, CEO of Nucor, the world's most productive steel maker. This company, however, is more famous for its management techniques than its product. John Correnti's eyes lit up when asked to describe his company. "We're a collection of the most highly motivated, highly productive people in the steel industry. We out produce our competition by almost five to one and we deliver high quality products. What makes us the best", Correnti explained, "is that we share our profits with our employees, we reward productivity, and we have almost no supervision. Everyone at Nucor is not only working for the company, they are working for themselves." Unfortunately not all companies have implemented the genius behind Nucor, but you can be assured that all employers want employees to show up on time, give it their best every day, be honest and loyal, and go that extra mile for the company. That is what having a strong work ethic is all about; that is what employers expect and deserve. Believe me, when employers look for people to keep or promote, they review the work ethic and productivity of their employees.

What's the Motivation?

Employee motivation surveys consistently indicate that we are motivated by three primary factors:

1. Recognition

2. Being part of the team

3. Fair compensation

These job satisfaction factors are listed in priority order. Most employers and their human resource personnel recognize the relevance of these factors and are alert to how prospective employees approach them in conversation. For instance, if an employee's major focus seems to be on compensation and benefits, he or she will not fare nearly as well as the employee who wants to know how he or she can do more for the company. Many of the more progressive American companies, including foreign-based companies operating in America, include their employees in the screening and interviewing process. Why? Because new employees will become coworkers, and coworkers can affect the productivity of the work unit or team. Often, a company unit or division is compensated by its productivity. In this environment a strong work ethic is essential for every member of the team. One TRANE Corporation division, located in Pueblo, Colorado, allows each work team to screen, interview, and employ persons for all open positions. This company really understands the significance of getting good employees and making them part of the organization.

An anonymous, but wise, author once said, "There's no traffic jam on the extra mile." Therein lies a golden opportunity for anyone seeking employment security or career advancement. Knowing about the law of 110 percent, you can design your daily performance to emphasize your positive work habits. If you wonder how you are doing, just compare your work habits and productivity with those around you. Do you work as long and as diligently as they?

Each new job or position is an opportunity to move past a former performance record and establish a better one. If you have had a good employment record, talk about it and be proud of it. If you are a first-time worker, resolve to give it 110 percent right from the beginning and let your supervisors know about your career plans. Ask the supervisors how you can best become a valued employee. They will be impressed.

Advice From The Pros

Al Allison, III is the Executive Vice President of Allison Fence Company in Charlotte, North Carolina. His business is of small to medium size and is labor intensive. Al is on a constant crusade of encouraging educational institutions to turn out workers with better work ethics. His company, like thousands of others across America, is desperate for workers who will show up on time, work hard, and be dependable.

Al says this about the importance of a good work ethic for peak performing employees: "A strong work ethic is extremely important and may be the most important factor in valuing an employee's worth to the company!"

Al has this advice to people who would like to advance and become invaluable: "Build a strong work ethic in your character, take charge of your health both physically and spiritually, and become competent in the product or service you provide. Seek balance in your life and always give more than 100 percent—you will become invaluable!"

Richard Kipp is Vice President for Human Relations, Okuma America Corporation, a major producer of industrial lathe and milling machines, is an expert in customer relations, employee relations, and training collaboratives. He is a national speaker about the importance of workplace skills acquisition.

Rick says this about the importance of work ethic for those who wish to advance and be secure in their jobs: "A good work ethic is very important for all workers. Employees need to be empowered, work with minimal supervision, and complete tasks in a timely manner."

Rick has this advice to employees who would like to advance and become invaluable: "Become proficient in your current job. Become knowledgeable about the company and share your knowledge with others. Participate in cross-functional projects when ever possible. Be positive and demonstrate loyalty to the organization. Be a self-starter and complete all assignments. Continue your education, work on interpersonal skills, and be willing to do more than your job requires."

Valuable employees generally become indispensable because they are productive, dependable, loyal to the organization and their supervisors, and they always seek to do their best! Take it from the pros and follow their advice.

Conclusion

Just as you expect your automobile mechanic to fix your car promptly and reliably for a fair price, employers expect to pay their employees a fair wage to be productive in a timely fashion, with quality work. If we, as workers, expect to be recognized for our efforts, appreciated by our coworkers, and compensated fairly, it's up to us to be the best at our jobs. It's up to us to put out 110 percent each and every day for the employer.

To become indispensable, you must emphasize your commitment to the company and underscore your strong work habits. Employers will continue to promote employees who will produce more for the company than their wages and benefits cost. Being honest, being a team player, getting to work on time, staying until the job's done, and being loyal to the company are all critical traits indispensable employees demonstrate to their employers.

Practical Advice

Projecting a positive attitude about life and about your career is essential. Communicating your enthusiasm for the job and the company is also important, and convincing employers that you have a strong work ethic is icing on the cake. The secret to making a great impression is to be all that you say you are. Be enthusiastic and positive, communicate well, and be a professional who is willing to give 110 percent every day.

Research tells us that those employees who are committed to the company inevitably get the promotions. You can illustrate evidence of your commitment to the company by doing more than your share, by placing yourself in positions of leadership and visibility, and by being a good corporate citizen. If you are involved in an interview for a promotion, a reference to your outstanding performance evaluations can also communicate that you are a good worker.

Finally, demonstrate your work ethic strengths when given the opportunity. Undoubtedly your coworkers and supervisors will ask you to tell about yourself. This is your cue to talk about your career goals and career successes. Everyday chitchat about your roots, your family, and your training helps build good relationships, but remember to talk about your enthusiasm for your work. Let them know that you enjoy working for a quality company where you can grow by helping the organization grow and that you want to be a team player with people who aspire to be the best!

Points to Ponder

1. Project enthusiasm.

2. Project integrity.

3. Project dependability.

4. Project cooperation.

5. Project competence.

6. Project diligence.

7. Project loyalty.

From This Day Forward

I will work harder and smarter than my fellow workers.

_____.

_____.

_____.

Chapter 4
Forget the Lone Ranger

If you don't believe in cooperation, just observe what happens to a wagon when one wheel comes off.

—Anonymous

THE FOURTH LAW FOR BECOMING INDIS-
PENSABLE IS BEING A TEAM WORKER!

In much of our early childhood we are taught to be competitive, and we are rewarded for out-performing our peers. We quickly learn to compare our performance to the performance of others, and our self-images are developed in this way. It is no wonder that teamwork comes as a shock to many of us as we enter the work environment that demands cooperation. With few exceptions, mostly in the arts, our jobs require good social skills and the ability to function as part of a team. Fortunately, most adults quickly develop a natural desire to be part of a team.

You can apply personal examples to verify the truth of the law of teamwork. Ask yourself the following questions:

Have I ever seen an effective organization that did not have a common purpose and good teamwork by its members?

- Is it possible for me to build a Delta II rocket by myself?

- How many loners have I really enjoyed working around?

- Would I rather work with a brilliant, but independent, coworker or an average, but collaborative, coworker?

Most employees are dismissed because of poor performance, right? Wrong. Most people are dismissed because of an inability to get along with others. Being caught in a downsizing effort is happening to thousands of workers every year. In many of these situations, the company uses seniority or job category to determine who is dismissed. In other situations, the dismissal decisions are left up to the supervisors. In these cases, you can be sure the troublesome employees, that is, the ones who are least cooperative, will get the ax first.

The Need to Cooperate

If you seek advancement at your current workplace, your reputation as a congenial team worker will be an important asset. Your initial task is to remove all doubt from the supervisor's mind about whether you are cooperative. If you have been uncooperative in the past, explain what you learned from the experience, and then state your resolve to never repeat the mistake. Having a great attitude, communicating well, and displaying a good work ethic are critical, but if there is a lingering doubt about your ability to fit in and work well with others in the company, you will be eliminated from consideration. It is also important that you are viewed as a person who contributes to the goal or vision of the organization. Whether you are the janitor, in accounting, or in middle management, remember that your real business is the business of the company. Every college employee is in the education business, everyone who works for a manufacturing company is in the manufacturing business. Everything you do at the workplace should contribute to the common purpose of the organization. Working harmoniously with others is critical. Cooperation is essential not only for achieving a work goal but also for keeping a happy, healthy work environment.

"Just how cooperative should I be?" you may ask. Your employer expects you to be as cooperative as it takes to get the work accomplished.

Several years ago my wife and I were interested in purchasing some land in central Texas. We were referred to a land Realtor named Big John and met him one rainy morning out in the hill country. Big John drove us out to the country off the back roads and onto a rarely used cow path. In shorter time than it takes to tell the tale, Big John's car slipped off the path into a four- or five-foot ditch. My wife and I learned about the consistency of the soil thereabouts after we trudged across a large rain-soaked field to a home owned by Mr. Austin. After we spent a pleasant hour with Mr. and Mrs. Austin, the tow truck finally arrived, and Big

John stepped out to make the arrangements. With a twinkle in his eye Mr. Austin leaned toward me and said, "You know Big John long?"

"No, sir," I replied.

"Well, me and Big John get along I reckon, but I do most of the gettin', you understand!"

We did not buy any land from Big John.

The point to the story? If you want job security and job advancements, be sure you do most of the gettin'.

Balance Between Task and Team

People will happily volunteer good references if they are deserved. Although most people are cautious about giving negative references, potential employers are very attuned to what is *not* said. If you are not sure about your ability to get along with others or whether you are perceived as a team player, reflect on your last or current job. Do people like you? Do your peers invite you to lunch? Do you share credit for tasks well done but accept responsibility for problems? Some people, particularly high achievers, are naturally more task oriented than team oriented. They tend to be loners at the workplace. Achieving a proper balance between being task and team oriented is a worthy goal. (An exercise in Appendix B will help you determine if you have a healthy task versus team orientation.)

I once worked with an absolutely brilliant man who could accomplish almost anything, as long as no one got in his way. People marveled at his passion for life and for his work. His peers appreciated his talent and admired his innovative ideas. His superiors—and I was one of them—loved his work as an individual, but were continually worried about whom he would offend next. Unfortunately, this talented individual could not work well with any ideas except his own. In consequence, he often felt it necessary to confront others about their "lousy" ideas and "stupid" opinions. Poor fellow, the last I knew he was jumping from job to job and being completely misunderstood and unappreciated.

The law of teamwork is fundamental to your success at becoming indispensable. Resolve now to talk less, listen more, criticize less, and praise more in every situation. You will feel better, and people will love you. Consider the best conversationalists you have known. Without exception they will be people who listen well and with patience. When you were a youth, getting the credit for some outstanding feat or performance was integral for the development of a healthy self-image. Some people are so insecure that they continue to strive for all the praise and all the glory, even when the achievement could not have been accomplished without the assistance of others. At the workplace, it does not really matter who gets the glory as long as the work team is recognized. It's the old "you reap what you sow" principle at work here. As you praise others, praise will be returned. If you want to improve your work situation, use this "listen more, praise more" attitude.

Being a team player also means contributing more than your fair share and being willing to try other people's ideas even when they make little sense. Your supervisors need to envision you as a contributing, amenable employee. You can communicate this notion by demonstrating an ability to get things done and get along with others. In this respect, keeping a sense of humor is important. Recent research indicates that people who can laugh at themselves and with others are more creative, less rigid, and more willing to try new ideas. Ninety-five percent of America's corporate executives will more likely hire or promote people with a sense of humor.

Advice from the Pros

Jerry Richardson, founder and principal owner of the Carolina Panthers NFL team, understands full well the importance of teamwork. As a former NFL player and as a highly successful restaurant franchise owner, this remarkable man believes that teamwork is absolutely essential to career and business success.

Jerry gives this advice to people who want to be the best at what they do: "Treat everyone with respect and be trustworthy. Be competent and eager to learn. Work hard, be harmonious, be a team player, and listen well. Finally, be positive and do your job the best you can, be dependable, and do what you say you will do."

Jim Morgan, CEO of Interstate Johnson Lane, a large brokerage firm located in Charlotte, North Carolina says: "Teamwork is critical at every level. We have learned over time that any employee who tends to think in the first person singular will eventually hold back our performance and will fail individually."

Jim has this advice for people who hope to become indispensable: "I would advise them to never underestimate the importance of people skills. Obviously, intelligence and common sense are critical ingredients for performing and managing, but relationship skills are even more critical for leading. An invaluable employee eventually leads his fellow employees in one way or another."

Conclusion

Employers and their human resource personnel know full well that an employee's ability to get along with others at the workplace is a critical skill. They know that a major part of their task is to support people who work well with others and contribute to the goals of the organization. During times of downsizing or promoting, these decision-makers will consider your ability to work well with others. The more you can convince them that you are a team player, the better your chances of being retained or promoted. To be sure, employers are interested in leaders, especially leaders who can motivate others, but make no mistake about the law of teamwork. Ignore this law and you will spend a lifetime looking for new employment.

Practical Advice

Whether you are a good team player does not really matter if you are self-employed or financially independent. But if you are like the rest of us, you should be honing your social skills continuously. Learning to listen, praising others, and trying out the ideas of others are skills we can all learn and continue to improve. Try them at home with your family and with your friends. Before long, unless you are already expert at these skills, people will wonder what has come over you. Better yet, as you make a consistent effort to improve these skills, they will become second nature to you just when you need them most.

During a crucial part of the Second World War, General Dwight Eisenhower was told that his command desperately needed second lieutenants. There were no junior officers to be had, but General Eisenhower solved the problem quickly by ordering second lieutenant field commissions upon soldiers who were Eagle Scouts. The general was aware that the Scouts would know about leadership and teamwork, both basic characteristics for military officers. The general knew that the first part of the Boy Scout Law, for instance, required them to be "helpful, friendly, courteous, kind." People who wish to become indispensable will do well to follow the same code. Being helpful, friendly, courteous, and kind just about wraps it all up if you want to keep and grow in your dream job.

Zig Ziglar, one of America's best motivational speakers and writers, reminds us that we can reach our successes if we help others reach theirs. It's the same at the workplace. We cannot expect to be successful alone. Come to think of it, even the Lone Ranger had Tonto to help!

Points to Ponder

1. Do most of the gettin'.

2. Learn to listen.

3. Learn to praise.

4. Try others' ideas.

5. Illustrate success through teamwork.

6. Be helpful, friendly, courteous, and kind.

From This Day Forward

I will be congenial and cooperative with my fellow workers.

_____.

_____.

_____.

Chapter 5
PS Is Critical

It is better to light a candle than to curse the darkness.

—Ancient Chinese Proverb

THE FIFTH LAW FOR BECOMING
INDISPENSABLE IS BEING A
PROBLEM SOLVER!

Employers are constantly on the lookout for people who can solve day-to-day problems. By adopting this law as a work habit, you will have no problems becoming indispensable. Setting and achieving career-related goals are always desired, but an employee who has the ability to solve problems is most valued by employers.

You can easily verify the truth of the PS (problem solver) law by considering the following questions:

- Which person would I rather have to take care of my lawn: one who cuts and trims only, or one who cuts, trims, feeds, seeds, and does whatever is necessary?
- Which automobile mechanic would I prefer: one who replaces parts according to symp-

toms, or one who searches out the cause before replacing parts?

- Which employee do I think would be most valued: one who says, "That's not my job," or one who says, "Let's see how we can fix this"?

Obviously, an employer prefers to employ people who have the confidence, ability, and personal incentive to solve problems. Anyone can dodge responsibility at the workplace by ignoring problems or by suggesting that problems are not his responsibility. However, those who want to do well in a career and those who never need to worry about employment will take on the challenges as they occur.

An Opportunity to Learn

Only shortsighted people view the job as a means to survive. Truly successful people see each assignment as an opportunity to learn and to become the best at that vocation. People with the "it's not my job" attitude will likely never find satisfaction at work or anyplace else for that matter. Supervisors are aware of people with such negative attitudes and they categorize them as dispensable employees.

As a college student, I worked full time at a television station as a technical engineer. I ran the cameras, audio board, film chain, videotape machines, and video board as assigned. I had to join a national labor organization to hold the position. One evening, while we were shooting a live commercial for an appliance store, a new television set began to slide off a shelf to the floor. A cameraman quickly steadied the television set whereupon a more seasoned employee chastised him. "That's not your job!" he bellowed. "Only the floor crew can touch things on the set. If you start doing things like that, they'll think they don't need a floor crew and we'll lose our jobs." You can buy into this attitude if you like, but it will be a violation of the problem solving law, and your chances for holding a good position and getting promotions will be severely restricted.

As a seasoned college president, I can spot problem solvers at my very first meeting with them. They have a special notion that they are part of the organization, and they delight in putting its goals above their own. They talk about solutions and opportunities to improve the college and its students rather than about problems or potential problems. They are optimistic, cheerful, cooperative, and customer focused. They recognize the importance of the position, no matter where it is in the organizational chart, and they take pride in it.

Unfortunately, most people generally take their problems to their supervisor rather than attempt to solve them on their own. This behavior does not make them bad people; they are just doing what most American organizations have taught them to do for the past one hundred years. The old organizational hierarchy often emphasized process over results. These days most of us in positions of authority are trying to develop a new work environment. We encourage people to take the initiative, to solve problems, and to make decisions on their own. The old hierarchical organizational model is no longer efficient or sensible. In short, we are looking for problem solvers.

Initiative, Imagination, and Ingenuity

Just how do you learn to practice the attributes of this law? First, you should clearly understand the organization's vision. What does the company really want to become or accomplish? Once you understand the vision or primary company goal, you should learn the parameters of your job, including how much latitude and responsibility you have for completing your tasks. Second, you should learn to exercise the three *I's*: initiative, imagination, and ingenuity.

Take the initiative when problems emerge. It is okay if it does not work out right the first time or even the second or third time. The point is that you are willing to take the risk, to be the leader in a difficult situation. Besides, opportunity seldom comes to us on a platter; it's usually disguised as a major problem. Problem solvers also use their imagination. They enjoy thinking outside the norm. They solicit input from others and from as many sources as possible. They never lose the childhood excitement of discovery. There is no substitute for ingenuity. Being resourceful and clever about finding solutions to problems for the ingenious is a creative process. Each problem or difficulty can be approached as an opportunity to be innovative, an opportunity to assist the company in reaching its vision.

Leadership

Leadership is a major part of the PS law. Leaders have the confidence to try new things, motivate people to work as a team, and accept the responsibility of failure. Leaders understand that failure is only an event.

Someone once said that if at first you do not succeed, you are running about average. No one succeeds at everything. Sure, Ulysses S. Grant was a great general and went on to become the eighteenth president of our country, but before the Civil War, he was unsuccessful in the military and in business. Yes, George Washington won the revolutionary war, but he lost the first eight of all nine battles of that war. As you resolve to become indispensable, try to demonstrate your leadership skills at every opportunity. Let the people you work with know that you are not afraid to take leadership roles in solving problems. Let them know you believe in sharing praise, but you can accept the blame alone if something goes wrong.

Famous Problem Solvers

Former President Franklin Delano Roosevelt exemplified the character of a problem solver. He served as president of the United States from 1933 until 1945. During that time, he led the nation through the worst depression and the most extensive foreign war in our country's history. His methods for stabilizing the country's economy and leading the war effort are still debated, but everyone concedes that he was a dynamic leader and an excellent problem solver. He faced formidable odds, including a physical disability, but he never ceased to use his resources to find solutions for the organization (country) he ran. He faced adversity with optimism and stress with unconcern.

Another famous problem solver received the Presidential Medal of Freedom in 1977, but he refused all cash awards for himself. Jonas Edward Salk created the polio vaccine at the University of Pittsburgh in

1953, and this terrible disease, which killed or disabled hundreds of thousands each year, has been virtually eradicated from the earth. Dr. Salk used all the resources and staff at hand to fix a problem for untold millions of people now and in the future.

Not all of us can become as famous as Roosevelt or Salk with the solutions we discover. But each of us, solving one problem at a time, is contributing to the betterment of the organizations for which we work, the economy, and ourselves. Most important, by assuming the character of a problem solver, we increase our chances for employment success.

Advice from the Pros

Employers the world over are interested in finding and keeping employees who can think on their own and use initiative, imagination, and ingenuity at work. The following executives offer this advice to any worker who aspires to be the best.

Ron Harper, Chairman and Chief Executive Officer of Harper Companies International, and his wife Katherine, President of Harper Companies, own and operate one of America's most successful and respected Flexography manufacturing organizations. They produce highly sophisticated inking cylinder equipment for the Flexography printing industry.

Ron has this to say about the importance of the ability and interest in solving problems at the workplace: "It is extremely important for peak performing employees to be able to solve problems. The best employees accept accountability, take risks, and take charge of problems. They generally consider their options and solicit opinions from co-workers and subordinates before moving forward."

Ron gives this advice to people who would like to be considered indispensable: "Read! Study successful managers and nurture a positive attitude. Take calculated risks, get involved, and go the extra mile every day. Honor your commitments."

Tom Moser, National Director for Consumer Markets for KPMG Peat Marwick, a nationally respected accounting firm says this about the importance of having good problem solving abilities: "It is very important to learn how to access relevant information quickly and to learn how to involve others in arriving at the best decisions."

Tom has this advice for people who wish to excel at their careers: "Learn how to work well in teams and complex organizations moving across departmental boundaries."

Conclusion

Employers are looking for people who will take the responsibility to solve problems. They are eager to employ people who will take the initiative to improve on processes, services, or production to help the company increase profits and reach its vision. Wise employees acknowledge the importance of the PS (problem solver) law and seize opportunities to demonstrate initiative, imagination, and ingenuity. Successful employees exhibit leadership skills by demonstrating belief in themselves and in the value of teamwork. Above all, successful problem solvers continually ask themselves how they can help the company improve.

Practical Advice

Let your supervisors know that you believe in solving problems as they occur. And when problems need to be bumped up the ladder, you will present some recommended solutions. Corporate America is pushing decision making to lower levels to achieve better efficiency and productivity. The demand for employees who think for themselves and are not afraid to look for solutions is increasing. Here in lies a great opportunity for you to become indispensable.

Points to Ponder

1. See problems as opportunities.

2. Project initiative.

3. Project imagination.

4. Project ingenuity.

5. Be a leader.

6. Believe in yourself (and others).

From This Day Forward

I will trust my instincts and attempt to solve problems at work as they occur.

_____.

_____.

_____ .

Chapter 6
Service Leads to Satisfaction

Those who bring sunshine to the lives of others cannot keep it from themselves.

—Sir James Matthew Barrie

THE SIXTH LAW FOR BECOMING INDIS-
PENSABLE IS BEING CUSTOMER FOCUSED!

We all like to be treated with dignity and respect, especially if we see ourselves as customers. Employers are acutely aware of this consumer expectation, and they desire to have customer-focused employees. Violating this service law will guarantee unemployment.

Human nature has not changed much over the years, and consumers today wish to be treated well, just as consumers of the first century wished to be well treated. You can verify the truth of this law by answering the following questions:

- Do I like prompt and pleasant table service when I dine out?

- When the cable television or telephone is on the blink, which would I prefer talking to: a recorded voice or a real person?

- When I have some questions about my child's scholastic progress, would I prefer a defensive or receptive teacher on the other end of the line?

If we really want to know what type of employee most businesses are looking for, we merely have to visualize someone who impressed us with service. Learning to treat others as we like to be treated is the secret to this service law.

Two Types of Customers

But I work in manufacturing or engineering where I seldom come into contact with customers, you may be thinking. Guess what? Your work will eventually come into contact with the customer, and it will affect the image of your company. Furthermore, you work with a host of internal customers each day. Most American workers have two major types of customers, external and internal.

External customers are the people or companies that purchase your products or services. Internal customers are those people you work with in the production of products or services. Each customer is equally important. Without good service to external customers, production will diminish, quality will suffer and your company will go out of business. Without good teamwork and cooperation at the workplace, production will diminish, quality will suffer and your company will go out of business. All employees of an organization, no matter what type of business, must be ever conscious of who their customers are and aspire to serve them well.

My wife and I recently visited a new neighborhood restaurant that had been highly recommended to us. We arrived on Saturday evening at six o'clock. The décor and ambiance was impressive. Waiters stood ready to serve throughout the dining room, but only one of twenty-three tables was occupied. "We'd like a non-smoking table for two," I told the hostess.

"Do you have a reservation?" she replied.

"No, We didn't realize we needed reservations. Besides'" I appealed, "it looks like you have plenty of room."

"I'm sorry," she replied firmly. "We only take people with reservations on Saturday evenings."

We left the restaurant and I'll bet the hostess (or perhaps the entire restaurant) is gone by now also.

The Boss as a Customer

Most employees understand that the boss is also a customer. They will go to great lengths to please him or her. In reality, each person they serve or work with deserves the same considerate treatment. It takes the cooperative efforts of everyone in a business to make the business profitable and effective.

The point of this service law is obvious. Employers are eager to get and keep people who value customer service and demonstrate the ability to be customer focused both externally and internally. Customer satisfaction equates to successful careers and job security.

Advice from the Pros

Learning to be customer focused with a service above self attitude will inevitably separate you from the common to the uncommon employee. Businesses depend upon customers for their very survival. Those workers who understand the vital importance of serving customers will become indispensable in the eyes of their employers.

Jane Cooper is the Chief Executive Officer for Paramount Parks, a national entertainment park organization that stretches across the United States. Jane has this to say about the importance of being customer focused for those who hope to advance and become invaluable employees: "It is very important that employees be customer focused. They must understand who ultimately pays them and why the company is in business (to make a profit)."

Jane has this advice for anyone who would like to become indispensable: "Demonstrate early on your level of commitment to the company. Seek out ways to expand your knowledge base either through the organization or through college. Show flexibility and adaptability. Focus on how you can serve the company and make it better. Finally, learn to manage your career and be aggressive in a professional manner."

Rick Priory is Chairman and Chief Executive Officer for Duke Energy Corporation, one of the world's leaders in energy production and innovation. Rick has this to say about the importance of customer service: "It is critically important for all of our employees to be customer focused! Customers and their satisfaction with our products and services are the very reason we exist."

Rick has this advice for those who wish to become indispensable: "Stay focused on the reason your company or organization is in business. Remember that your company has to satisfy customers and make a profit for owners. Each employee plays a part in achieving these objectives."

Jim Amos is a successful author and businessman who has been sought by some of the country's most respected corporations. He is currently President and CEO for MAIL BOXES ETC. This international company is expanding rapidly and has become a household word. Jim has this to say: "You cannot be a peak performer without being customer focused. There are three primary value disciplines that a company can embrace today. One is product quality, a second is operational excellence and the third is customer intimacy. As an example, Sam Walton embraced operational excellence through his distribution system to build Walmarts and Sams. At MAIL BOXES, ETC. we embrace customer intimacy as our primary discipline. Today you must be competitive in two of these disciplines and world class in at least one. Regardless of the position he or she holds, every associate deals with customers either inside or outside the organization. People skills are imperative. The differences between organizations are the differences between people."

Jim's advice to people who want to become indispensable is: "Today there is no such thing as job security. However, there is employment security. This can only come from becoming more valuable to the organization. To advance and become more valuable you must become a lifelong learner and teacher. This requires that you read material and associate with people who can help you grow and then share that knowledge with others. When given responsibility, take charge. There is something important going on all the time. Look for it. Whatever your job, regardless of how menial it may appear at the time, do more than is required."

We're all In the Service Business

All indispensable workers understand the importance of service to others. Whether they are directly serving external customers or working with coworkers, these successful people know the value of service above self. To them, cheerful service becomes a way of life, an attitude of endless commitment to helping others, a distinguishable part of their identity. I can assure you that supervisors clearly know which of their subordinates is customer focused.

"But I'm in the manufacturing business, not the service business," you may say. Baloney. We are all in the service business, no matter what we do or where we do it.

"But I am a loner. I don't like people much, and I cannot change the way I am," you may protest.

Hogwash. We have the freedom and the ability to change an attitude about anything anytime we wish. As we change attitudes, our behaviors change, and we profit because of this conscious effort at self-improvement. And the best part about conscious attitudinal change is that it becomes unconscious behavior after a short while. In effect, we can reprogram our attitudes at will. Now that is real freedom!

Putting the service law into practice must become a way of life. It means that we continuously think about the needs of others and not just about the literal accomplishment of a job assignment. A colleague directed her maintenance people to put one hundred chairs underneath some trees on our college campus in preparation for an annual retirees' picnic. She was aware that standing for long periods would be prohibitive for many of the older people. Fortunately, she checked on this activity just before the event was to begin. Her subordinates had indeed placed the chairs under the trees, but they left them in the double-tiered storage racks. Their commitment to customer service was less than ideal. These workers had performed the literal task as assigned, never thinking about setting up the chairs for the college's esteemed guests. The men failed to understand the principle of the service law. "Service above self" is a good motto for people who want to find and keep good jobs.

Conclusion

Employers must have satisfied customers and satisfied employees. Employers are looking for people who genuinely care about serving others, both paying customers and fellow workers. Employers seek employees who understand that customer service is a virtue. Employers truly value employees who apply a customer service attitude eight hours a day, five days a week. Finally, astute job seekers will recognize that their service to others and their ability to get along with others are the best methods for job security in this insecure world of work.

Practical Advice

Remember, employers desire customer-focused employees. You can have the best credentials, the best skills, and the best intentions, but if you cannot serve your external and internal customers well, you'll be of little use to your employer. Being customer focused means more than just having a cheerful attitude. It means having a true commitment to serving others. In the world of work, serving others means helping others meet their needs and achieve their objectives sometimes in spite of your needs or standard operating procedure.

Putting the service law into action means thinking about the intent of the work assignment and doing your best to accomplish the goal as opposed to simply trying to get by with the least amount of effort. People recognize and appreciate service-oriented people. Your reputation for service to others follows you wherever you go. The next promotion may well depend on someone's recollection of how you treated him or others around him.

Points to Ponder

1. Service to others is a virtue.

2. Employers value customer-focused employees.

3. Customers include everyone, inside as well as outside the company.

4. Customer satisfaction equates with job security.

From This Day Forward

I will be the most customer-focused employee in my work group.

_____.

_____.

_____.

Chapter 7
Results, Not Process

Our grand business is not to see what lies dimly at a distance, but to do what lies clearly at hand.

—Thomas Carlyle

THE SEVENTH LAW FOR BECOMING INDISPENSABLE IS BEING RESULTS ORIENTED!

In their milestone book *In Search of Excellence,* Tom Peters and Robert Waterman described America's most successful corporations as having a "bias for action." The employees of those companies created the corporate environment the co-authors described. In other words, the most successful companies have people with a bias for action, employees who are interested in results more than processes.

You can verify the truth of this successful career trait by asking yourself the following questions:

- When my child or I last needed medical care, was I more concerned with completing the health insurance verifications or with seeing the doctor?

- Have I ever been given the run-around by a company when I needed repairs on something still under warranty?

- Did I ever need to pick up the laundry, but the cleaners didn't have it ready?

Most of us have experienced the frustration associated with one or all three of the above illustrations. As consumers, we are interested in immediate attention, no lectures, and no run-around. Is it any wonder that employers value on the lookout for action-oriented, results-seeking employees?

If you have ever had to wait for an auto part or for a certain fabric to be available, you can understand why employers need workers who produce things on time. If customers cannot get what they want in a timely manner, they will take their business elsewhere. Employers understand this basic relationship between producer and consumer, and they keep and promote people who also understand this principle.

Getting Things Done

Employers desire customer-focused employees who can get things done. A cheerful, engaging attitude is nice, but it is not enough to become indispensable. To become invaluable, you have to convince the employer or supervisor that you can get things done and that you will help the company make more money than your total cost of employment. In short, you are an enterprise that will accomplish tasks assigned in a results-focused manner. Indispensable employees understand how to work within the parameters of company policies and procedures to complete tasks in an exemplary fashion.

How busy you are and how busy you look have little to do with actual productivity or accomplishment. A person can be busy all day and all week, but never come to closure on anything of value to the organization. Work has a way of expanding to fill the time allotted for it. A number of productivity studies have proved this principle. The best employees consciously focus on accomplishing assigned tasks to the very best of their ability in a timely manner. These employees seem to have an intuition for being productive and they are highly appreciated by their employers.

We've all witnessed people whose desks are overflowing with papers, reports, and books. Usually, their office chairs and tables are also loaded with paperwork. They think this office demeanor projects how important the job is and how hard they work. In reality, their office condition projects disorganization, confusion, and insecurity. Either they are thoroughly disorganized and inherently messy, or they are attempting to boast about how much work they do. In either case, such a display indicates that these people are process-oriented as opposed to results-oriented employees. Results-oriented people are eager to finish tasks and move the paperwork along. Results-oriented people have a strong need to close out projects and tasks and move to the next challenge. Their desks or work areas are generally kept clean and uncluttered to be prepared for the next task.

Character Flaws

Some people are simply lazy. For some inexplicable reason these folks would rather put off doing the work than jump into it. They are almost never productive. Even if they manage to get a job, their chances of keeping it are slim unless they have some type of labor protection. Such behavior is wasteful for the company and for the employees. Believe me, employers can spot lazy people faster than a speeding bullet.

I have known many lazy employees in my career, but the worst ones are almost always very intelligent. Such people work harder to keep from working than to do their assignments in the first place. I have yet to find a good explanation for such behavior, but I have learned to identify these people with great accuracy. Most of them would make excellent employees if they could eliminate that one character flaw. The point? Companies or organizations exist by providing products or services. All employees must carry their share of the load if the employer hopes to stay in business. If you hope to keep a cushy job where you do little work, you may as well throw in the towel now. You will be found out. Ignoring this law of action and results is one of the surest ways of becoming dispensable.

There is one exception to this law, yet this exception is diminishing in the United States. Strong labor unions often protect workers from losing their jobs for most anything except violence or direct insubordination. As a young television station cameraman in the sixties, I well remember being criticized by my union "brothers" for working too hard. Their reasoning was that the company would expect everyone to be that productive if I kept working so diligently. They often advised me to carry a hammer around the studio and just look busy. That unfortunate experience illustrates how peer-imposed work behaviors can be destructive to initiative, ingenuity, and self-worth. If you intend to become indispensable, you must be a results-oriented person who understands that personal productivity is the best job security and be a person who takes pride in helping the employer be successful.

Companies fail for many reasons, but the surest road to failure is for them to be noncompetitive because of poor production or poor service. All employees of a company can lose their jobs if a few peers fail to recognize that their ability to achieve results affects the profitability of the entire company. As you seek to become invaluable, project an image of a results-oriented, hardworking, enthusiastic person who looks for solutions, not excuses.

Everyone can find excuses for not getting the job done. Some people become experts at the art of excuses. They generally blame others, blame the equipment, blame the customers, blame the company, or blame some condition beyond their control for poor performance. In truth, we generally have no one to blame but ourselves for poor performance. Do not listen to others who help you find excuses or tell you some task cannot be done or is unreasonable. Above all, do not listen to yourself when you begin to think negatively. Successful professionals learn to focus on completing tasks, no matter how difficult, with a positive mental attitude. When you work, avoid espousing excuses just as you avoid using profanity. Your reputation must be impeccable. You never know who talks to whom about you and your career opportunities.

Change Is A Part of Life

If you have become process-focused try to shift that focus toward solutions and results. Not so long ago people were outraged to hear that a long distance bus driver made an eighty-nine year old woman get off his bus on a lonely highway at night when he discovered she had a small dog. Company policy was being violated and this process-oriented champion did his duty. By using such poor judgment, the bus driver created a public relations nightmare for his company.

As president of a college, I often go to where our customers are being served to get an eyewitness account of our services. On one such occasion, at the beginning of a new semester, I saw two very long lines in the bookstore. Some lines are to be expected during this time since all students are buying new books and supplies for their classes. To my amazement, the students were standing for twenty or thirty minutes in the first line to present their book list and receive their books from a clerk. The students then stood in another line for twenty or thirty minutes to pay for the books! I asked for an explanation from the bookstore manager, but I was less than satisfied. After making a few suggestions and hoping that some creativity would emerge from the manager, her response was, "But that's how we always do it." You can imagine how much confidence I gained in that employee at that moment.

You can stay results oriented if you constantly remind yourself of your primary responsibility. With rare exception, every employee's primary purpose is to produce quality products or services for customers. When the process interferes with this primary purpose of your job, you have an obligation to change the process within your purview or request a change in the processes outside your purview.

In all problematic situations you should ask yourself two basic questions: (1) Is it good for the customers? and (2) Is it good for the company? If the answers are in the positive and your solution is legal, you will seldom be wrong, even if a particular procedure or process says otherwise.

Becoming process oriented is generally nonproductive and unbelievably bureaucratic. Take a look at the Internal Revenue Service if you want to experience process orientation at its worst. The IRS code alone has more than seven million words, most of which are left to interpretation! Becoming process oriented is a trap that all professionals should avoid.

Advice from the Pros

Being results oriented and prone to action is a common characteristic among successful employers. It is natural for employers to value these same characteristics in the people they employ. John Correnti, President and CEO of Nucor Corporation, the nation's second largest producer of steel products, exemplifies this law.

When asked how important results orientation is for peak performing employees, he had this to say: "Being results oriented is very important. Peak performers will do best when management gives them goals, holds them accountable, then stays out of their way."

John gives this advice to people who wish to excel in their careers: "Always give more than is expected. Never, never give up on any assignment or duty. Be a good listener and learn how to communicate on every level, lowest to highest."

Kris Friedrich, founder and CEO of Money Mailer, the largest mail-based advertiser in the country, is keenly interested in attracting and keeping high performance employees. He has this to say: "It is extremely important to be results-oriented and it is the key to balanced success. Don't just be focused on your own goals because you may reach your own, but fail to meet the goals of the organization. The results must be viewed in the whole scheme of the plan. Do not be self-limited. Have specific performance standards and stick to them."

Kris's advice to people who desire to be the best is this: "Begin with a dream then set goals. Take action and set realistic time frames in which to reach your goals. Be visible! Take risks! Step up to the plate and out of the box!"

Conclusion

Companies and people are valued for their ability to get things accomplished. Consumers appreciate and are willing to pay for quality products and extraordinary service. Employers keep and promote employees who understand the importance of being results oriented, people who have a natural desire to be productive and focus on the needs of the customer. Indispensable people will put this law of action into practice day after day. A distinct asset of a professional is a solid reputation for getting things done.

Practical Advice

Projecting a work ethic that includes a bias for action and an interest in achieving results will pay big dividends for people who desire to be promoted. Successful people avoid any behavior on and off the job that could damage their reputation as effective and valued employees. Laziness, negative thinking, and a bureaucratic mentality should be avoided at all costs. Remember, employers value people who have a strong need for closure and who enjoy getting things done in a timely and professional manner. Employers consciously seek, keep, and promote employees who think for themselves and focus on solutions rather than on problems.

Points to Ponder

1. Have a bias for action.

2. Focus on results.

3. Have a strong need for closure.

4. Build a good work reputation.

From This Day Forward

I will work for results and attempt to change processes that interfere with results.

_____.

_____.

_____.

Chapter 8
GETTING IT TOGETHER LAW

Order is light, peace, inner freedom,
self-determination: It is power.

—Henri Frederic Amiel

THE EIGHTH LAW FOR BECOMING INDIS-
PENSABLE IS GETTING IT TOGETHER!

Accomplishing your work in an effective manner is the essence of the getting together law. One secret for always being effective and productive is to be organized at work and always seeking your long-term career goal. If you have no career goal or specific job objective, you will likely be unhappy with the work you are doing. If you have a job objective but do not develop or work a plan to achieve it, you will fail. No one can reach a goal unless it has been clearly identified and it is accompanied with a plan for its accomplishment. In short, if you want a dream job, get your act together.

You can easily validate the truth of this law by considering the following questions:

- If I wanted to drive from Atlanta to Denver, would I consult a map?

- Would I rather have a well organized or a disorganized teacher for my six-year-old?

- Do I prefer to fly with pilots who file flight plans?

Most people spend more time planning for a family reunion or a Fourth of July picnic than for their careers. Just a little planning can help you take advantage of the getting it together law. Planning and diligent effort are the keystones to career and financial success.

Staying Organized at Work

Have you ever felt like you were spinning your wheels at work and not really accomplishing very much? If you haven't felt like this, you are truly unusual. Everyone has days where things just don't quite fit together; the computer breaks down, the right people are not available, or the equipment needed to finish a job is missing. In spite of these inevitable frustrations, indispensable employees always seem to find a way to get the job done. How do they do it? By being organized and staying focused on the important tasks to be completed.

The following is a simple formula for being organized and effective at the workplace:

1. Prioritize tasks

2. Think logically

3. Do one thing at a time

4. Evaluate for improvement

I once knew a CEO who spent more time writing a monthly newsletter than leading his organization in accomplishing its essential tasks. He failed to concentrate on the important aspects of his job and was replaced within a year. Common sense in prioritizing your daily work and emphasizing essential tasks will help you rise above your competition.

Thinking in a logical manner is also an attribute of valuable employees. A checker player who seldom thinks beyond one or two moves doesn't win many games. A person who works the same way is seldom very productive.

Once a sequence of tasks has been mentally reviewed, it is important to stay focused on one task at a time. If we constantly remind ourselves of how big or impossible a job is, we will ultimately become discouraged and fail. Good time managers understand that you can only eat an elephant one bite at a time. Therefore, stick to each task until it is finished, before worrying too much about the next one.

Finally, indispensable employees understand that when it comes to quality and time, there is no finish line. These valued employees regularly evaluate their work in order to improve upon it. They continuously evaluate their work informally by thinking about ways to improve. They often evaluate their performance in a more formal manner by seeking input from peers, supervisors, and customers.

If you employ these tactics for becoming more organized, you will soon be selected for more responsible leadership positions and you'll be well on your way to becoming indispensable.

Advice from the Pros

Being well organized is prized and respected by employers, regardless of their business field. Charles Davidson, President and Chief Executive Officer of J. A. Jones Construction, a multi-billion dollar, international construction corporation, has this to say about the importance of being organized: "It is extremely important to be organized at the workplace. Eighty percent of what we do is the necessary work that maintains the momentum of our business. Being organized allows us to perform this necessary work efficiently."

Charlie has this advice for people who would like to advance and become invaluable: "Lead a balanced life. Commit significant portions of each day to the development of your spiritual, intellectual, physical, and social well being. An absence of growth in any one of these four lifelong functions can adversely affect the other three."

Katie Tyler, a recent businesswoman of the year in Charlotte, North Carolina owns and operates a successful mid-sized construction company. She responded that "being organized isn't important, it is essential!" She offers this advice to people who wish to advance and become invaluable: "Write an essay of how your life will be when you become who you want to be. Include a reference to your company and how you will interact with it. Also describe your family life and personal life, then share this essay with everyone involved, including your boss. This will help to make your life's plan into reality."

Tony Fortino, a highly successful automobile dealer, real estate entrepreneur, and small businessman in Pueblo, Colorado agrees that being organized is very important. His advice to people who want to excel at the workplace is: "Do your job with enthusiasm and a positive attitude. Always learn as much as possible about your job and your career."

What Is Your Career Potential?

Choosing a perfect job or career can be frustrating and confusing. After all, your long-term success and satisfaction in the workplace depend upon this critical selection. Fortunately, many people eventually gravitate toward a career they enjoy. Many others, however, drift from job to job and never find one that is truly rewarding. Still others find themselves caught in a downsizing industry and must select a new career field to become employable.

You can take the guesswork out of the career selection process by understanding your job-related interests, values, and abilities. As you compare probable careers or jobs to your interests, values, and abilities, the identification of a career category eventually becomes evident. Consider exceptional athletes or scholars. They first discover their unique interests and abilities, then they select the sport or academic area they most value. By capitalizing on their basic interests, abilities, and values, they practice to become exceptional. The same principle holds true for people who successfully match their special interests and skills to jobs that allow them to flourish.

Further, you should choose a career path that you really value. Frankly, it does not matter what others think you can do. What matters is what you think and what you truly wish to do with your life. I am in my fourteenth year as a college president, I have a doctorate, have written ten books, and I have achieved national acclaim in some educational circles, yet two high school teachers told me that I was "not college material." You can be anything you wish to be if you want it badly enough and are willing to work hard.

Most people believe that IQ, grades in high school, and socioeconomic condition are the primary predictors of their future success. They are wrong. The most accurate predictors of future success include a moral character and a career vision with the desire and self-discipline to pursue that vision. Your personal motivation to reach a goal or to succeed at a vision will determine your career success. Your consistent zeal for and focus on the goal are paramount if you hope to achieve your personal career vision. For this reason, select a career goal that you truly value and fully expect you can accomplish. If you neither value nor expect to reach the goal, you will fail.

In the early seventies, I taught two young college broadcasting students whose academic conditions were dissimilar. John's performance in the classroom was below average. Gary's academic record was exemplary. John's grades dropped so that a colleague counseled with him. "It is obvious you are not very interested in your studies, John. Just what is it you would really like to do?" my fellow teacher asked. "I'd really like to make music," John replied. We suggested that he should try it. A few years later John Cougar Mellencamp hit the charts as one of America's top rock and roll stars!

From my first meeting with Gary, he told me he was going to be the voice of the Indianapolis 500 and would be a television network announcer for auto racing. His grades were always outstanding, and he was graduated with a degree in broadcasting without a slip. A few years later, Gary Lee was recognized throughout the country as the ESPN anchor for auto racing.

What attributes propelled both young men into their nationally recognized careers? It was not their academic success or their economic status. The vision or career goal and persistence in achieving it were the attributes that made them so successful. They both set a goal that they highly valued and expected they could reach.

Of course, you must see yourself clearly and objectively. It is unrealistic to think you can become a professional baseball player just because you want to be famous and make a big salary. Even Michael Jordan, one of the greatest NBA players of all time, tried to make it in professional baseball but failed to excel in that sport. It is equally unrealistic to think you should become an astronaut unless you're willing to get the education and training required for that competitive career. If you exaggerate or minimize your interests or abilities, the result will likely be unpleasant. Be true to yourself when you select your next job objective or long-term career goal. Appendices C and D provide career assessment and career goal setting activities that will help you identify the career areas most suited to your interests, values, and abilities.

Take note: Before you can accomplish anything, you must truly want whatever is to be accomplished. Motivation is linked directly to what you value plus your belief that you can attain it.

As the U.S. adjusts its goods and services to be competitive in the global marketplace, jobs will be changing by type and skills required for at least the next ten years. American businesses cannot compete with the cheaper labor forces in less developed countries to do the standard assembly jobs of the past. Mexican and Malaysian workers can assemble piece goods, including clothing, at less than half the cost demanded by American labor. However, niche market areas in manufacturing lend themselves to American assembly because we have the automated technology or the exclusive knowledge base to out-produce foreign labor. Further, the demand for American computer software and for health and consumer services is increasing rapidly. In short, the United States will excel in highly technical jobs and in selected services jobs through the year 2005. By the way, college degrees are important, but not as essential as they once were. Today's employers are mostly interested in skills and performance.

Developing a Plan of Action

People never accomplish much without thinking about what they want and how to best go about getting it. Since achieving your career goal is a job in itself, it is prudent to develop a plan and follow it. This plan should be action oriented. Achieving your career goal should require you to take a series of actions, from writing your resume, preparing for promotions, and determining the most effective path to success. The following components are recommended for an effective action plan:

1. Research needed skills

2. Determine best path to success

3. Develop a list of people who can help

4. Develop a plan for networking

5. Develop a follow through system

The first step in developing a plan toward achieving your career goal is to determine what job skills are necessary. You can talk to your supervisors, someone who has a job at the level you aspire to reach, or you can do some formal research. Most libraries have access to Internet databases and other resources like the <u>Occupational Outlook Handbook</u> that will help with this task.

Determining the best path to achieve your career goal is to first, resolve to become an indispensable employee, then talk with people in the field to identify the most common path successful people have followed in that particular career. In the broadcasting industry, experienced sales people, rather than engineers or program people, usually become general managers. College presidents have most frequently come from instructional ranks, rather than from finance or student services.

Making a list of people to talk with can be a valuable exercise, but only if you talk with them. Most people love to talk about themselves and enjoy being asked for advice about their career field. Be bold and visit with people who can give you good advice.

Networking, especially at your workplace, is extremely beneficial and a simple follow-up habit of sending thank you notes is always wise.

Networking Effectively

Once you have a clear career goal and a plan for achieving it, you will increase your chances for success by learning to network with anyone and everyone who can help in your career pursuits. Networking is a career boosting skill that you can learn to do well. The secret is to become good at making friends. The purpose of networking is to help you get leads on advancement opportunities and job-promotion interviews. Networking can also lead to formal and informal references, and it can provide a more thorough perspective as you move up your career ladder. In effect, each person you talk to about your career goal has the potential to become a career consultant to you at no cost. Networking can be fun, exhilarating, and effective if you are prepared. The best people to help you achieve your career goal are usually the people you work with every day. Your peers and supervisors can become the foundation for your career success. Job hoppers often think they are climbing the career ladder. Unfortunately, they fail to build a base of supporters and they end up building their careers on a house of cards. As friends and professional associates help you climb your ladder to career success, remember them and stay in contact as much as possible. In the end it is your professional reputation and personal relationships that will make you successful. After all, companies don't promote people, people promote people. One last suggestion, as you get the opportunity to help others achieve their career dreams, consider it as a privilege, not an obligation.

To be an effective networker, you should take every opportunity to be with people and to win friends who can help you. Becoming a good communicator is relatively easy if you follow this formula for successful communication: listen, listen, and listen some more. Most of us have two ears and only one mouth. God had good reasons for this configuration. Invariably, study after study on communication indicates that the best communicators are those who have the patience and wisdom to listen. That means listening before responding, avoiding interrupting the speaker, and listening some more. This one communication skill can do wonders for your job search activity. You should also ask how you might be able to help those with whom you are networking. Building relationships is the key to this job search activity.

Occasionally, you will meet with people who do not speak freely. You need to find out about their interests as quickly as possible and focus on these things. If you are meeting someone on referral or for an interview, do some preliminary homework. Get a biographical description from someone who knows him. In this way you can get a feeling for his interests, and you can discuss your commonalties. The closer someone can connect with you, the more likely he will support you.

While in conversation, do not miss the chance to ask people for advice about your career goal. Asking for advice is a sign of self-confidence, a sign of respect for the other person, and it is flattering. Once they give you advice, you must make every effort to use it and tell them how it helped. This situation will reinforce your relationship, and they will develop a greater commitment toward your career success. It should go without saying that you should send a handwritten thank-you note to everyone who helps you even a little bit.

Finally, you should make a conscious effort to become as literate as possible with the issues surrounding your targeted objective. You will become infinitely more believable as you become conversant about your sought-after position. Read everything you can find about your career field, and talk, listen, and listen some more to people in that profession.

Conclusion

Employers are looking for self-motivated employees who know what they want and are well organized. Successful people embody these characteristics to reach their career goals. Envisioning a long-term career and staying focused on immediate job tasks are the first steps toward achieving the getting it together law. Learning to plan and network effectively are two additional important steps toward becoming successful in your career. Being well organized projects confidence, reliability, and an impressive reputation to employers. You can display all the behaviors represented by the other eleven laws for getting a job and still be unsuccessful if you are disorganized. Ignoring this law will be disastrous.

Practical Advice

Getting organized—and staying that way—is the surest method for becoming indispensable. When you do get to the important interview for your next promotion, you will have a definite advantage because you will have it all together and that will be evident to the interviewer.

Points to Ponder

1. Organize each workday

2. Set a career goal

3. Develop a career action plan

4. Follow the career action plan

5. Learn to network

From This Day Forward

I will plan my career strategy based on my ultimate career goal.

_____.

_____.

_____.

Chapter 9
Put Your Best Foot Forward

Early impressions are hard to eradicate from the mind.

—Jerome

THE NINTH LAW FOR BECOMING INDIS-
PENSABLE IS PUTTING YOUR BEST
FOOT FORWARD!

Once you have determined your career goal and
have developed a plan for getting it, you must focus
your attention on the job of selling yourself. You must
learn to put yourself in the place of your supervisors
and employer. They will be looking for evidence of the
twelve essential laws for becoming indispensable as
described in this book. They will be looking for someone
in whom they can have confidence, someone in whom
their expectations can be met.

You can verify the truth of this law by asking yourself the following questions:

- When I last bought an automobile, was the
  credibility of the salesperson important to
  me?

- When I last chose a bank, a physician, or a veterinarian, did the reputation affect my choice?

- When I visited my child's school, how long did it take to get an impression of his or her teachers?

Certainly, a person's credibility, reputation, and impression are important to us when we consider purchasing goods or services from them. The same principle is true of employers and people in general. Self-esteem exhibits itself in many ways, and a healthy sense of confidence is important. But the impression you make on others is critical when you seek to become the most appreciated employee in your company.

As you network within the workplace, consider everyone you come into contact with as potentially helpful in the achievement of your job goal. Always put your best foot forward. This is a small world, and your reputation depends on what other people think of you. Each person you meet, especially in the workplace, presents an opportunity for you to build a stronger and stronger reputation. Your reputation is your most powerful asset for becoming indispensable.

The First Sixty Seconds

The first sixty seconds of an encounter with a stranger are most lasting! There is much truth in the adage that we never get a second chance to make a first impression. Human beings are social beings. We exist in a world where our social experiences, that is our relationships with others, form the essence of our lives. All of us, employers included, have learned to develop instant opinions of other people based upon the way we perceive them through their reputations and personal demeanor.

Your objective is to sell your worth to your employer on a daily basis, not by taking credit for every good accomplishment, but by giving your best every day. In a real sense, you should view yourself as an individual enterprise. In this way, your skills and talents will translate into value for yourself and your employer. The critical first sixty seconds of each customer contact, each peer contact, and each supervisor contact is your most important asset for job security and advancements if you know how to put your best foot forward.

Be Mentally Prepared

First things first. Many coaches are fond of saying to their athletes, "Get your head on straight." The same advice holds true for becoming indispensable. You must project confidence, enthusiasm, and trustworthiness. Your comfort level in promotion related discussions and interviews will increase in direct proportion to your preparation for these events. To this end you should spend some serious time talking about your career goal and how you plan to achieve it through your commitment to the company.

Your career goal is a vision of where you would like to be and what you would like to be doing with your life five, ten, and even twenty years from now. Your ability to clearly explain your career goal or next job objective to your employer will affect your chances for getting promotions and achieving your career goal. You need to know where you want to go in your career and how your career interests can help the employer meet his or her needs. For example, your career goal is self-centered, but the way you relate it on paper and during interviews should be employer or company centered. Employers want to know what you can do for them, not what they can do for you.

Once an applicant spent five minutes in an interview telling me why the job she had applied for would be so important for her career aspirations. She never understood that I was more interested in what she could do for our organization than what we could do to further her career. Some people believe they are entitled to a job or a promotion. But believe me, an entitlement attitude will guarantee employment failure.

Essentially, your next advancement or job objective should state the type of position you are seeking and the contributions you hope to make to your employer. Unfortunately, a typical job objective looks like the following: *I am seeking a responsible sales position that provides opportunities for advancement,* or *I am seeking a challenging supervisory position in operations engineering.*

Both examples are applicant centered. They do not tell the employer what you can do for him or her.

A better advancement or job objective would be: *I am seeking a responsible sales position where my experience, energy, and diligence will produce higher profits for my employer,* or *I am seeking a supervisory position in operations manufacturing where my engineering and management experience can be used to increase corporate productivity.*

Be Spiritually Prepared

Being prepared mentally is essential, but it is often not enough. Indispensable workers are usually at peace with themselves, and they have enough faith in God and in themselves to sustain them during any work situation. Further, they accept advancement rejections professionally with the understanding that rejections should not be taken personally. Finally, they have the heartfelt assurance that another advancement opportunity will soon evolve and that in the long run, all things happen for their good.

You can boost your spiritual preparation by associating with other persons of your faith and by reading Scripture. Two of the best methods for increasing spirituality are encouraging others and personal prayer. Most supervisors and employers easily recognize the self-confidence that usually results from a solid spiritual foundation. Employees who are spiritually as well as mentally prepared have confidence and naturally put their best foot forward!

Be Physically Prepared

Becoming indispensable will require all the physical stamina you can muster. Each job has its share of stress and sometimes strenuous activity. Getting and staying in the best physical shape possible will heighten your chances for career success. If you are not now in proper physical condition, there may never be a better time to exercise and eat a proper diet.

Your appearance can be your best asset or your worst liability when you interact with people, especially supervisors, at work. Your first and continuous impression will make a dramatic impact on them. The time to assess your overall visual and vocal impression is now—not a day or two before the opportunity for a promotion occurs.

It is sad but true; people treat you as they perceive you. Your first visual and verbal association with others will set off a whole series of judgments about your character and abilities. Even your handshake will project volumes about you. "But that's not fair," you may retort. Perhaps it is not fair, but people the world over process information and draw conclusions from that information the same way that you evaluate car salespeople, physicians, or teachers.

Your dress, hygiene, breath, posture, grooming, body language, facial expressions, and speech contribute to your ability to make good impressions. You should display an attitude of alertness, vitality, and confidence under all situations associated with your work. That includes informal times when people observe you without your knowledge.

You are well advised to develop your appearance according to that expected of people in the position you most desire. Successful professionals pay close attention to their appearance. Their clothing, hair presentation, and accessories are consistently appropriate for their work. Basically, they present a conservative appearance that does not detract from the information exchange process. Successful people also employ good posture, make frequent eye contact, and smile easily. Of course, they also converse easily and succinctly. Anyone who aspires to become a valued employee should be his or her best at dressing, posture, grooming, and articulating at all times.

Your speech should be natural with appropriate volume and clear diction. Having to exert a special effort to hear or understand you will make a negative impression on people. Certainly, eye contact and moderate smiling are essential elements for making good impressions. Don't play any power games by demonstrating your assertiveness or your ability to dominate. Be yourself, be courteous, be professional, and be in the best physical shape possible. Remember that you will be making impressions with everyone you meet, and you never know who or what group of people can help you reach your career goal or goal to become indispensable.

Be Socially Prepared

Your whole attitude should be to make as many friends as possible. People help people, and they usually help ones they know and like. The more friends you have, the better your chances for keeping a job and getting the promotions you want. Smiles, good listening skills, and thank-you notes become valuable tools in the socializing process.

One other thing to consider: careers are competitive by nature. As you attempt to project yourself as the most productive, customer friendly employee in the company, ask yourself this question: *"If I were to compete with myself for the advancement I'd like, what would I do?"* The answer to this question will help you compete better for that new promotion.

Be Prepared for Tough Questions

Putting your best foot forward also means being prepared to answer the tough questions when you interview for a career advancement. Interviews generally create high anxiety for interviewees, but that anxiety can be reduced if you anticipate the tough questions and prepare for them. Most of these questions are designed to help the interviewer discover your values, work ethic, attitude, and ability to work with others, as well as your communication, analytical, and work-related skills competence. You should approach each question honestly and straightforwardly, always emphasizing one or more of the twelve essential laws for becoming indispensable. Some standard questions include the following:

- Where have you worked in the past (i.e., describe work history)?

- Why do you want this new position?

- How well have you performed in your current position?

- Where do you want to be in five or ten years?

- What can you tell me about a career accomplishment?

- What can you tell me about a career disappointment?

- How do you usually handle angry people?

- Why are you the best person for this position?

- If I called your current supervisor, what would he or she tell me about you?

I interviewed a candidate for a high-level position who spent a full fifteen minutes describing his career in detail. I finally had to interrupt him to ask my second question, which concerned his career goal. His answer to that question was equally lengthy. He ended by stating that he would really like my job as president of the college and that he imagined I'd be retiring in a few years. Since I was still in my forties, he scored a zero for diplomacy. In any event, the applicant would clearly talk his coworkers to death. He did not get the job.

Conversely, another applicant for the same high-level position gave the shortest answers in history during the interview. She was very self-assured and was obviously well prepared for my questions. In fact, she was too prepared because her answers were like rehearsed sound bites for a camera interview. I tried to get her to relax and show me who she really was, but to no avail. There was no warmth in the personality, and her answers were so curt, I felt she was hiding something. She did not get the job either.

Advice from the Pros

Presenting a strong professional image is a hallmark of successful people. Dale Halton, President and CEO of a large Pepsi Cola Bottling franchise in Charlotte, North Carolina epitomizes this characteristic and expects the same from her best employees. She says that a professional image is very important for employees who wish to advance. "They set the tone for all those under them and need to represent our company in a professional manner at all times." Her advice to people who would like to become invaluable is: "Work hard and be honest. Represent your company in a professional manner at all times and be open to seeking new opportunities and challenges."

J. Frank Harrison III is the president and CEO of a Coca Cola Bottling franchise headquartered in Charlotte, North Carolina. He says professional image is very important because "Right or wrong, people are initially judged by how they dress, their demeanor, etc." His advice to people who wish to advance is as follows: "Continuously work on the following areas:

1. Your character

2. Your skills

3. Your trustworthiness

4. Your listening ability

5. Your ability to communicate at all levels."

Conclusion

Putting your best foot forward is a sure way to achieving employment success. Employers promote people they feel good about, people they like. Employers listen closely to managers and to candidates when making promotions. Your ability to make a great impression before, during, and after the interview will determine whether you get the position. The first sixty seconds of the interview are critical. Everything about you, especially your attitude, communication skills, and personal demeanor, plays a part in how the interviewer perceives you. Be mentally, spiritually, physically, and socially prepared for the interview. Anticipating interview questions and having honest, believable answers will carry you to success.

Practical Advice

Projecting a positive, friendly attitude with a professional demeanor is a foolproof formula for job-keeping and advancement success. People promote people who are productive and likable. Successful employees know how to be on their best behavior at all times, including during the interview and they think of themselves as enterprises. Indispensable employees do not feel entitled to positions, but they are willing to earn them by being their best before, during, and after their interviews.

Points to Ponder

1. Learn to sell yourself.

2. Know what you want.

3. Be mentally, spiritually, physically, and socially prepared.

4. Recognize that the first sixty seconds are most important.

5. Be prepared for the tough questions.

From This Day Forward

I will be my best in all social and work situations.

_____.

_____.

_____.

Chapter 10
Learners: A Priceless Commodity

The education of a man is never completed
until he dies.

—Robert E. Lee

THE TENTH LAW FOR BECOMING INDIS-
PENSABLE IS BEING AN ACTIVE LEARNER!

Employees who cannot or will not continue learning
risk becoming permanently unemployed. Transitional
workers who are not active in learning new skills and
new work behaviors will likely remain unemployed for
a long time.

You can verify this law by asking yourself the following questions:

- If I owned a secretarial service and one
  employee refused or could not learn to operate the new, more efficient word processing
  software, would I (a) allow her to keep using
  the old software or (b) replace her with an

employee who could operate the new software?

- I am interviewing equally qualified applicants, but one shows evidence of active learning throughout the career. Which applicant would have the edge?

- Which type of worker is most valued by the employer: a passive, methodical person or an active person who is eager to learn new work skills and techniques?

The correct answers are obvious, but they illustrate the point. The American workplace is changing rapidly, and the academic, technical, and behavioral skills required for workers in all fields demand continuous learning. Your willingness to gain new skills to be more productive at work represents the active learner law. Sometimes the learning curve, or demand for new skills acquisition, is steep (fast), and sometimes it is rather flat (slow). In either case, we are in a new environment that requires increased learning and new skills throughout our lifetimes as workers.

As a young boy in the 1950s, I was curious why our neighbor, a grizzled and reclusive older man we called Fuzzy, seemed to be so poor, yet never worked to earn any money. Our family of ten always had plenty to eat, but everyone worked. "Fuzzy has a rough way of it, son," my father explained. "You see, he used to be a well digger, but modern technology came along, and he didn't keep up with it, so he was pushed out of a job." That incident made a lasting impression on me. If anything, the changing technologies at the workplace today are occurring at lightning speed compared to the changes in the early fifties. We no longer live in a predictable world where we can expect to earn a living by the sweat of our brow. We no longer live in a world where we can expect to work for the same company in the same basic position until retirement. Just as poor Fuzzy was pushed out of a job for not learning new skills, today's workers are suffering the same fate with greater frequency. The tragedy is that it is not necessary to lose employment because of a skills deficiency.

The opportunity to learn new academic, technical, or social- behavioral skills has never been better. Most employers recognize the importance of keeping a well-trained workforce and encourage or even provide training for their employees. Community and technical colleges offer almost unlimited training opportunities, private training firms are bountiful, and many universities are expanding their outreach efforts. In short, if you need to acquire new skills, there is little excuse for not doing so.

American businesses spend $30 to $40 billion annually to train their employees. Business leaders expect to employ highly trained workers, but they realize that they will need upgraded training as technology and the competition change. Here are three emerging trends in this regard:

Management is providing more training for all workers.

Employees are managing themselves with less supervision.

Public higher education institutions are increasingly providing work-site education and training.

By the year 2000 more than 90 percent of all jobs will require some education beyond high school, 23 million people will be employed in technical vocations, and nearly 85 percent of all American workers will need upgraded skills training to perform in their current positions. Learning has become a lifelong process, and we must continually upgrade our skills.

Shifting Workforce Skills

In the late 1970s and the early 1980s, national policy makers identified a skill shortage among American workers, especially young workers entering the workforce. Study after study indicated that the United States was last or near the last in academic preparation among the industrialized nations of the world. In 1983, *A Nation at Risk,* published by the United States Department of Education, made ominous predictions about the country's condition if our K through 12 educational system did not dramatically improve. We were losing our role as the most productive country in the world, and we had just slipped from the lowest to the highest debtor nation in the world. In the late 1980s, additional federal papers were published, including *America's Choice: High Skills or Low Wages* and *Workforce 2000,* which outlined the critical need for America's workers to become better skilled. Meanwhile, a Massachusetts Institute of Technology study on the loss of manufacturing jobs reported that if we wanted to live well as a nation, we had to out-produce our foreign competitors. We had emerged into a globally competitive society, and the requirements of our businesses and their workers have never been the same.

The mandate for all workers to become academically and technically skilled is clear. The requirement for people to continuously increase their skills is equally clear. The responsibility for the acquisition of these skills is yours. I had an employee who refused to learn how to operate our new electronic mail system because she claimed she was too old to learn about such things. I also had an employee who still dictated in person to his secretary, refusing to use advanced technology for dictation or the composition of correspondence. Both people were great individuals with strong work ethics, but their productivity suffered because they refused to learn new workplace skills. I can assure you that employers everywhere in the U.S. are most interested in self-motivated employees who recognize that learning new skills is a necessary part of the job.

Today, our public K through 12 schools are doing better than they were in the late 1970s. Our students are scoring about average on academic tests compared to other industrialized nations. American workers are more technically proficient due mainly to the accessibility of training through community and technical colleges. Yet the skill shortage among American workers continues. There is a skill breach between worker preparation and employer expectations. Workers who can fill this gap and meet the needs of the employer will become invaluable.

If you wish to be among the most sought-after candidates for any position, learn the behavioral and technical skills sought by employers, and make sure your prospective employer knows you have learned them. Of course, employers expect certain minimum academic and technical proficiencies, but their primary interest is in finding and keeping employees who exhibit behaviors that contribute to the success of the business or organization. As American businesses have learned to reduce supervision and increase employee autonomy, those most valued have positive attitudes, communicate well, solve problems, and have a good work ethic. As modern employers attempt to push decision making to the lowest levels, they seek employees who take initiative and know how to make decisions. In effect, the skills most valued by employers are behavioral. That is precisely why ten of the twelve essential laws for becoming indispensable are behavioral in nature!

You cannot ignore the final two laws, however. Having the specific academic and technical skills and the experience to do a job well is critical in most situations. As you pursue your long-term career goal, you must identify what specific knowledge and skills you will need to be successful. You will need to develop an action plan to achieve the education required and become committed to it. People in your local college or skills training center will be more than happy to help you with this entire process.

By applying the active learner law, you will have a significant advantage over your competitors in getting the position you want. Certainly, employers look for evidence that you have a healthy appetite for learning new academic and technical skills. More important, they look for evidence that you have an enthusiasm to work effectively within the organization, can assume responsibility, and have the ability to motivate others to high performance.

Assessing and Addressing Your Basic Deficiencies

Employers are interested in things you know, can do, and feel. They know that no one person excels in everything, and everyone can improve academically, technically, and attitudinally. They respect employees who have assessed their deficiencies and are doing something to correct the deficiencies. If an employer perceives that you have a positive attitude, she will admire you and be more likely to promote you.

I recently interviewed the perfect employee. The gentleman spent so much time telling me how wonderful he was; he talked himself out of contention for the position. People who think they are perfect have at least two major problems: (1) they will lie to you, and (2) they will lie to themselves.

Once you have decided on your long-range career goal and have developed a plan to reach it, discover your academic and technical deficiencies by matching the academic, technical, and physical skill requirements of the career goal to skills and abilities you already possess. Most public libraries and all college libraries will be able to help you with this task. The United States Department of Labor has numerous publications such as the *Dictionary of Occupational Titles* and the *Occupational Outlook Handbook* that will be useful in this exercise. (Appendix E provides some activities in this regard.)

Discovering social or attitudinal deficiencies is more difficult because we are reluctant to tell others about our shortcomings, and most of us are protective of things that affect our self-esteem. An honest review of your social behavior and personal attitudes can be accomplished by conducting an assessment. You ask (or have someone else ask) your former supervisors, peers, and subordinates to evaluate your team building, team playing, communication, and work ethic skills. Some useful personality assessment instruments are available at your local college, university, or career center. These personality profiles can be very helpful in identifying behaviors that come naturally and ones that you'll have to work on. A review of past performance evaluations will often provide the information you need to objectively assess your behavioral deficiencies. Sometimes a candid visit with a good friend can be revealing.

In any case, smart employees seek to discover their deficiencies and resolve to correct them through a personal development plan that may include college courses, professional seminars and training, apprenticeship training, and a conscious effort to change work behaviors. You need to identify your deficiencies and work hard to eliminate them, but do not despair about them. You can accomplish almost anything if your desire is strong enough.

Many famous people have overcome serious deficiencies to be among the best in their career field. Winston Churchill held the lowest academic rank in his elementary school. General George Patton was dyslexic and flunked mathematics at the U.S. Military Academy. Remember Helen Keller? You get the point.

One final note. Many companies provide learning opportunities for their employees. Some, like the McDonnell Douglas Corporation, have developed "learn to earn" programs where employee paychecks are increased in proportion to increased learning. You will do well to ask an interviewer if such learning opportunities are available with the organization. When a prospective employer understands you are interested in self-improvement through staff development opportunities, you'll have one more credit on the right side of the ledger.

Advice from the Pros

Bill Dowdell is President of the Flexographic Technical Association, a highly respected national organization for the flexography (printing) industry. He has worked all over the country with hundreds of employers and offers this insight to the importance of continuous learning: "Learning new skills has two significant and invaluable benefits for the employee and the employer: first, it indicates an ability to *continually improve* within the present function that is so important for a company to remain competitive. Second, in today's technical environment, radical changes in manufacturing and service industries demand the incorporation of processes that enable a company to remain in business and compete in a leadership position."

Bill's advice to people who wish to advance is: "Demonstrate the ability to perform the job position in the next level of the hierarchy, and learn the jobs related to, but not necessarily in, your immediate sphere of responsibility."

Gene Rackley, a partner of Heidrick and Struggles, a nationally respected executive search firm, has worked with thousands of corporate executives and thoroughly understands the labor challenges they face. He and his company believe that all outstanding leaders must have a high appetite for knowledge and learning. "More importantly," Gene relates, "they must actively continue improving their knowledge and skills to be peak performers."

Gene gives this advice to people who wish to excel in their careers: "Base your life on unshakable values. Be self-motivated, confident, organized, enthusiastic, and develop good interpersonal communication skills. You'll become as indispensable as possible!"

Conclusion

Applying the active learner law is essential for keeping a job and advancing in today's changing workplace. Successful professionals are willing and eager to correct skill deficiencies in the academic, technical, and behavioral dimensions. Your ability to communicate to supervisors that you are aware of your strengths and weaknesses and that you constantly work toward improvement is important. The goal of this tenth law for becoming indispensable is to convince your employer that you are able to learn new skills and perform in new ways, and that you always have the company's interest at heart.

Practical Advice

Discovering new knowledge, new technical skills, and better workplace behaviors is an exciting part of life. As you work your way through this process of self-improvement to optimize your career opportunities, remember that learning is truly lifelong. The very business of life should include constant growth academically, technically, and attitudinally.

Points to Ponder

1. Learn to earn.

2. Keep your skills current.

3. Demonstrate your skills.

4. Assess and address your deficiencies.

From This Day Forward

I will actively engage in professional development activities that will help me reach my career goal.

_____.

_____.

_____.

Chapter 11
How to Gain SATS

Few things are impossible to diligence and skill.

—Samuel Johnson

THE ELEVENTH LAW FOR BECOMING
INDISPENSABLE IS HAVING THE PROPER
ACADEMIC AND TECHNICAL SKILLS!

You can verify this law by reviewing your past experience with job hunting. In most instances, you were required to meet some minimum educational and/or technical skill levels before being qualified for the job; that is, you had to have "specific academic and technical skills" (SATS). You can verify this law by looking at the help wanted ads in your newspaper, in Internet job banks, or in a trade-specific journal that lists job openings. Inevitably, all meaningful jobs require a minimum educational level, and most include specific technical skills.

According to the U.S. Department of Labor (1995), the earning power of high-school dropouts is 20 percent less than that of high-school graduates. In 1992, a male college graduate out-earned the high-school graduate by 83 percent. Further, job losses for unskilled workers are nearly four times the job losses for college graduates. Certainly not all good career positions require a college degree, but there is a clear statistical advantage for those who increase their academic and technical skills. In fact, research tells us that only twenty-one percent of the jobs in the year 2005 will require a four-year degree. However, about seventy-five percent of jobs in that year will require specific technical skills usually associated with two-year occupational degrees.

It will be prudent for you to consider the usual minimum academic and technical skills required for the career goal you have targeted. Reading the requirements of similar positions in newspapers, journals, and computer networks will give you a representative idea of what academic and technical skills or degrees and certificates you will need to compete for the positions you want. However, current supervisors and people who already hold positions you hope to get will be your best source of information regarding position requirements within your organization. As mentioned in chapter 10, other sources of information for this research include the United States Department of Labor publications *Dictionary of Occupational Titles* and *Occupational Outlook Handbook*. These publications should be available at any community or college library. In any event, you will not even be considered for new positions if you do not meet the minimum requirements. Human resource personnel make the first cut of candidates by looking at which ones meet the minimum position requirements.

Just how do you prove that you meet the minimums? Most people cite or list their highest academic year or degree earned in addition to any formal training certificates. Unfortunately, many people fail to provide a complete listing of their academic and technical skills. By thoroughly examining your specific academic and technical skills and listing them convincingly on the position application or citing them in an interview, you will reap the benefits of this essential law.

Identifying Your Academic and Technical Assets

You can accomplish a detailed review of your academic and technical skills with just a little effort, and this effort will increase your esteem with your employer. During a formal job selection process, your cover letter, resume, and application may be the only things that represent you. If you do not make it through the screening and get an invitation for an interview, you are wasting your time. Therefore, your cover letter, resume, and application must be professional and thorough in every respect. More important, your goal should be to convince the screeners that you exceed the minimum academic and technical requirements. For example, if the job calls for a high school diploma, you should list it and add anything and everything of significance that demonstrates you exceed the high school diploma. Prior experience is important, also, but that is the subject of chapter 12.

During an informal promotion process, you may be casually interviewed or simply mentally reviewed by your supervisor and those who will make the selection. In either case, be sure they know you are interested in the position and that you exceed the minimum academic and technical requests. I was once passed over for a dean's position, even though I had the proper credentials and reputation, because I didn't express a clear interest in the job.

To identify your academic and technical skills, make a list of the following topics:

- Formal education and training

- Informal education and training

- Workplace training

- Hobby and volunteer service skills

Under each category, list things related to your overall academic and technical skills expertise. You will be surprised how knowledgeable and skilled you really are. In the formal education and training category, you should list the highest level of school or college you have achieved thus far. You should also list any vocational or technical certificates or training you have earned through high school, trade school, college, or the military. Also, list your military occupational specialty; this information is important to a screener of applications. If you have a college degree, list your major and minor areas of study. The more information you give, the easier it is for an application screener to get a thorough profile of you. Keep your application succinct but informative.

Informal education and training should include any major professional development activities you have experienced on your own, through your church, Scouts, or any other non-work-related organization. Seminars on time management, personal management, or interpersonal communications would be of interest to the application reviewer. First aid, emergency medical technician (EMT), and cardiopulmonary resuscitation skills indicate your interest in others and underscore that you value continuous learning.

Sometimes it is not so much the specific skill that impresses the application reviewer, but the fact that the person has experienced something in common with you. It is human nature for one EMT-certified person, for example, to favor another EMT-certified person when all other qualifications between applicants are equal.

As a self-supporting college student, I was once desperate for a full-time job. A fraternity brother was finishing his degree and leaving his position at a local television station, and he encouraged me to apply. I had absolutely no experience in the field, and I was somewhat intimidated by the prospect of working there. Nonetheless, I applied for the position, and I got it largely because my two interviewers liked me. One of them had belonged to the same fraternity when he was in college, and the other was very supportive of the Boy Scouts of America. I am an Eagle Scout. Both men knew of the character, leadership, and citizenship skills that were provided through our common experiences and that gave them enough confidence to hire me and train me with the specific skills needed for the position.

Professional development experiences at the workplace are often the most relevant to the new position being sought. Think back through your employment history, and list things you learned on the job, either through company-sponsored training or through workplace experience. Do not assume that the application reviewer automatically knows the set of skills you learned from reading your prior job titles. The skills associated with job titles vary a great deal from organization to organization. Either list a brief description of these work-related skills in the work history section of the application, or list them under the education and skills section. For instance, perhaps you were a machinist. Does this mean that you know how to program computer-controlled lathes and milling machines or that you operated these machines? As a graphic artist, are you skilled in computer-aided design software, and have you developed any software of your own? As an accountant, did you learn to write auditing or operational manuals? Did you receive training in customer relations, teamwork, occupational health and safety administration, or aid for disabled Americans? The specifics of meaningful skills in addition to your prior job titles are important.

Finally, people who promote others are interested in your hobbies and non-work-related interests because they paint a more comprehensive profile of who you are. These avocations are also a source of specific academic and technical training that most people overlook when competing for new positions. Some of your pastime or volunteer activities may give you the edge in the screening process. Obviously, a listing of trivial skills is unwise, but I know of many self-taught computer graphics experts who expanded their job prospects because they knew how to lay out and produce newsletters. Others increase their value to employers because they have published newspaper columns or magazine articles. Your volunteer service as a fund-raiser, for example, will be of particular interest to most employers. Employers are always interested in people who are committed to helping others, but they may be particularly impressed that you know how to raise money. I know of many people who moved into professional sales or development positions as a direct result of their volunteer efforts in fundraising.

From personal experience, I can tell you that employers and job screeners actively look for ways to screen out applicants so they can get to a manageable number of people to interview. The first thing screener's look for is the minimum education and training levels required for the job. Next, they look for the required experience minimums. I have never discarded an application for being too thorough, but I have pitched hundreds because they did not provide enough information to pique my interest. Certainly you should be succinct, but the law is clear: If you short change or understate your academic and technical skills, you will be handicapped in the job advancement process.

Confronting Your Academic and Technical Limitations

To advance and meet your growth potential, you must have mastered the basic skills of reading, writing, and mathematics at the tenth-grade level or higher (most daily newspapers have a ninth-grade readability level or lower). A high school diploma or equivalency is essential. You must also be proficient in the new basic skills that include information-gathering skills, problem-solving skills, the ability to communicate and work well with others, and computer keyboard skills. Many companies now require applicants to prepare their job applications by computer, thereby demonstrating their keyboard competence. If you are deficient in any of these areas, I implore you to take a positive step toward a better future by enrolling at your local community or technical college. If you get the proper skills and keep a positive attitude, you will most likely advance in your company.

I can provide hundreds of personal examples of how adults with poor basic skills and low self-esteem have overcome their deficiencies and are now enjoying personal, career, and financial success. Let me tell you about one woman who was a single parent with three children and was living in a homeless shelter when she decided to change her life. With help from our community college and social services, she succeeded in getting a high school equivalency degree, scored a straight A average in her pre-nursing courses, and earned her registered nursing license in three years. She now holds a good job, supports herself and her family, and fully recognizes that people can improve themselves academically if they so desire. One of the most courageous people I have ever met was an illiterate sixty-four-year-old African-American man whose goal was to be able to read and write. After three months of literacy training and with tears of pride streaming down his face, he told me he had just written notes on every Christmas card to his family and friends. Do not be afraid to learn; be afraid not to.

Do not worry about how long you have been out of school. Today's colleges are full of students in their forties, fifties, and sixties! Without the proper academic and technical skills, your chances of becoming indispensable are minimal. Even if you now hold a good job, you probably will not keep it long if you have academic and technical skills deficiencies. Learning has become a lifelong process for today's workers, and all future learning depends on your mastery of these basic skills.

Advice from the Pros

Bob Hanley directs a multi-state training center for the General Motors Corporation. Bob says that having the proper academic and technical skills is most important! The right person with the right education and technical skills who thinks, as well as accomplishes tasks outside the box, is invaluable." Bob has this advice for people who wish to advance: "Develop top-shelf communication skills, both written and oral. Listen to all suggestions and concerns and act on them. Develop a career path or plan with specific goals that enhance the skills required to meet the mission statement of the organization you wish to work for. Develop people skills that enhance and empower."

Philip J. Kirk is president of the North Carolina Citizens for Business and Industry, a powerful business organization that helps influence state policy regarding business. He is a former state legislator and serves as Chairman of the board for the state Department of Instruction. Phil believes that "strong academic and technical skills are essential, but without a positive attitude, a desire to excel, and a desire to learn, their value is diminished."

Phil's advice for people who hope to become indispensable is this: Be positive, have a good attitude, and work hard, but don't become a workaholic. Spend time with your family."

Conclusion

Knowing the specific academic and technical skills needed for your ideal position is essential. If you do not possess or fail to represent these specific skills to your employer, your chances of career success are slim. Identify job-relevant academic and technical skills through an assessment of your formal, informal, workplace, and hobbies-volunteer services training and experiences. Honestly confronting your academic and technical limitations is necessary if you hope to take full advantage of the SATS law.

Practical Advice

Matching your specific academic and technical skills to ones required for each position leading to your career goal requires serious attention. First, your position application materials and your supervisor's knowledge of your skills should make it apparent that you not only meet, but exceed, the minimum educational and technical skills required for the job. Second, if you know you have academic limitations related to the occupational position you desire, do whatever it takes to eliminate them or risk becoming dispensable.

Points to Ponder

1. Know your academic and technical capabilities.

2. Record your academic and technical strengths on application materials.

3. Deal with your limitations positively.

From This Day Forward

I will use my academic and technical skills abundantly and work to improve them continuously.

_____.

_____.

_____.

Chapter 12
Been There, Done That

All experience is an arch to build upon.

—Henry Brooks Adams

THE TWELFTH LAW FOR BECOMING INDIS-
PENSABLE IS EMPHASIZING YOUR
PRIOR EXPERIENCE!

Many positions require prior experience as a minimum job qualification. This is entirely within the
rights of the employer. Usually, a prior experience
requirement is necessary because of some productivity
or safety issue. Whatever the case, you must resolve to
get the experience needed before competing for positions which require prior experience. If you lack the
experience needed for advancement, do not waste your
time or the employer's time by applying. Even if you
bluff your way into the position, your ruse will likely be
discovered, and your reputation will be tarnished.

You can verify the truth of this law by asking yourself the following questions:

- Would I employ an inexperienced house painter?

- Would I rather have operating on me an experienced or an inexperienced surgeon?

- If I was responsible for managing a construction crew, would I prefer that they be experienced?

Making the Most of Your Experiences

The issue of prior experience is fundamental to most employment positions. In practice, most employment notices list minimum education and experience requirements that applicants must meet before being considered for the position. But many people ignore these minimum required qualifications and apply anyway. My human resource people tell me that a full 50 percent of applicants for professional positions do not meet the minimums and are automatically discarded. First, they could not handle the position's responsibilities, and second, a qualified applicant would have an excellent court case if an unqualified applicant got the job. The point? Do not waste your time or the application screener's time by competing for a position without meeting the minimum requirements.

The good news is that you may have experience that qualifies you for more positions than you suspect. More important, a thorough survey of your employment history and work-related experience will help you demonstrate experience beyond the minimum position requirements. If you identify an open position that fits within your career goal, look carefully at the minimum academic and technical requirements to be sure you meet or exceed them. Next, look at the minimum experience requirements and assess your experience in the area. Begin by listing all direct work-related experience whether it was from a full or part-time job. Then consider all other relevant experience. For instance, any exposure in the retail market or work with people may qualify as experience in sales and customer relations. The six months you worked in a fast-food restaurant, the time you sold products door-to-door, and even your paper route can apply. At the very least, you could mention your experiences to demonstrate your versatility in sales and customer relations. If you work in the health professions, your Red Cross CPR certification, your Scout merit badge, and your volunteer work at the hospital add to your credibility and may be considered equivalent to on-the-job experience. The secret to the experience law, however, is to use the extra experiences to help you exceed the minimum requirements and to demonstrate your versatility.

One of the best methods for gaining the experience needed for career advancement is to leverage your opportunities through volunteer service or exhibit a desire to improve within your current place of employment. Several years ago, while I was president of a college in Colorado, a middle-aged instructor told me he had entered the education field after working for many years in industry. He was most interested in industrial recruitment and customized training for business and industry. I explained that he would need some specific experiences in those areas before he could be considered for such a position and that no jobs were currently open. He quickly volunteered his services in anything related to this area of the college's activities and requested the opportunity to sit in on one of our company training negotiations. My people were so impressed with his ability to strike a rapport with industrial leaders, he was soon invited to go on an industrial recruitment venture. Within a year, our director of industrial recruitment and customized training took a job out of state and guess who was promoted? Today, this person is the chief operating officer for a college campus of his own.

When you list your prior experience, whether in a cover letter, on a resume, or on a job application, do not exaggerate or stretch the truth. Once an employer even suspects that you are less than completely honest, you will be dropped from consideration. I interviewed a well-groomed, articulate woman for a highly responsible position. The minimum experience required for the position included five years as an administrative assistant to a chief operating officer. Her application indicated that she had such experience. During the first three minutes of the interview, I discovered that she had been only a clerk to a chief operating officer. End of interview.

When competing for a job promotion, it is appropriate to mention your indirect experience as a team member or as a participant in a work activity as long as you do not present it as if you directed the project. Employers are interested in keeping and promoting people who have high integrity and the ability to work with others. You should tactfully communicate your contributions to the company that added real value. If you worked on a project that saved the company money and time, be sure the employer knows it. If you received a merit raise or a bonus for service beyond usual expectations, be sure to mention that, also. Communicate anything that will help the applications screener or the interviewer develop a more comprehensive profile of you as an exceptional employee.

I am not suggesting that you boast about your contributions, but never take it for granted that decision-makers know anything about you. Annual performance reviews and monthly or quarterly reports to your supervisors provide excellent opportunities to blow your horn in a professional manner.

Your employer needs to understand your knowledge base in terms of workplace needs. What valuable work skills have you learned on the job or through your hobbies and volunteer service? Have you learned to become a good communicator, a persuader, a team player, or a leader? (Appendix F provides an exercise that can be helpful in this discovery process.) The point here is to learn to describe yourself in language that employers understand and consider relevant to their needs. As an employer, I listen for self-descriptors such as "enthusiastic," "committed," and "customer focused" when I talk with employees. To describe yourself as "having five years of experience in sales" is one thing. It is much more meaningful to the employer, however, if you describe yourself as "a creative, loyal, and energetic professional with five great years of experience in direct sales."

Coping with Rejection

Inevitably, we all experience failure in getting a promotion or position we want. Rejection from a position you really want and need is always difficult. However, do not take it personally. Many of the decision-making variables are completely out of your hands. Besides, a better opportunity usually appears later on.

Most people can relate personal examples of a failure producing greater success. I once applied for a college presidency because a former colleague encouraged me to do so and because we were interested in returning to Texas where many family members lived. The move would have been lateral in nature, but I thought it offered some new career opportunities. I was selected as a finalist and my interview went so well, the governing board chair asked if I would accept the position. I replied that I would, but he had one more candidate to interview and, in fairness to the college and the other candidate, I advised he should hold the last interview. Much to my astonishment, the board hired the last candidate without a word of explanation to me. My wife and I were crushed emotionally. I learned two good lessons from that event: (1) never delay accepting a job if you want it, and (2) most things happen for good. Less than six months later I was recruited to be the president of one of the largest and most respected colleges in the country!

Just meeting the qualifications of a position does not entitle you to it. Over the years I have received scores of letters, phone calls, threats, and even civil rights complaints from people who thought they were discriminated against because they met the minimum requirements for a job but did not get it. My advice is to avoid the show of anger. You will burn a bridge unnecessarily, and you will develop a reputation as a person with an entitlement attitude. The Constitution of this country does not guarantee anyone a job. We have to earn jobs or create jobs for ourselves. By following the twelve essential laws for becoming indispensable, you will dramatically increase your chances for getting the positions you want in a timely fashion.

Advice from the Pros

John Georgius, President of First Union Corporation, one of the nation's largest banks, clearly understands the importance of experience in becoming a peak performer. In fact, his organization has an extraordinary commitment to providing experience and skills training to its employees via the First Union University. John will tell you that getting that first job is important, but getting broad-scale experience with many aspects of the organization separates great employees from good employees.

John has this advice for people who hope to become the best employees possible: "Be a team player with a positive attitude. Keep your skills updated and learn as much as possible about your company or organization to increase your value."

Katherine Harper, co-founder and President of Harper Companies, a large manufacturing firm that specializes in inking cylinder equipment, believes that there is no substitute for solid work experience. "All work experience is important, but experience that is directly related to your current job and to your career goal is always best. Employers value employees who are the most versatile and can work in a variety of positions within the organization."

Katherine offers this advice to people who would like to become indispensable: "Decide what you want to become, develop a plan to get there, and work hard. Be enthusiastic about your work, help others achieve their goals, and be loyal to your company. Look for ways you can do your job better and learn as much as possible about your work. You will become invaluable."

Conclusion

Getting a promotion involves assessing all your assets, including what you know, believe, and can do. The experience law relates to all three of these basic dimensions. The closer you can relate your work and work-related experiences to the needs of your employer, the more likely you will become a respected and valued employee. Do not bother wasting time competing for positions where your experience does not meet the required minimums. When you are qualified for a better position, do not neglect to cite or list indirect work-related experience in the applications material. Flaunt your experience in a descriptive manner that relates to the workplace needs of employers. Demonstrating a positive attitude along with your experiences, of course, is essential.

Practical Advice

As you assess your direct and indirect employment experiences, emphasize what you have contributed and can do for the company. Remember that no one is entitled to a job. We earn positions by selling our skills and abilities to others, or we create positions for ourselves. Use all of your prior experience to move up the career ladder within your company. After gaining experience in each position, use it to propel yourself into another promotion. You are an enterprise, and you will always be in a state of becoming; that is, you should always be a professional in transition, looking for new experiences and opportunities to advance your career. That is what all committed career professionals should be about. There is no finish line. That is the exciting part about working now and into the twenty-first century!

Points to Ponder

1. Assess your direct and related work experiences.

2. Learn to emphasize your experiences.

3. Promote your experiences in workplace language.

4. Take advantage of opportunities for new work-related experiences.

From This Day Forward

I will emphasize my life and work experiences during job promotion interviews.

_____.

_____.

_____.

Conclusion

Downsizing and new employment requirements have become commonplace in the United States. People who recognize that they are enterprises, fully capable of setting goals, solving problems, adapting to change, and achieving career success will survive handily. People who desperately seek employment security and believe they are entitled to a good job with high wages will be unhappy and generally unsuccessful in their careers.

Fortunately, by applying the twelve essential laws for becoming indispensable, you can expect to be successful at securing new career advancements and achieving promotions throughout your lifetime. By reading, understanding, and applying the principles of this book, you have every reason to feel secure with yourself and your ability to achieve your career goal. The only true job security rests with your belief in yourself, a clear career goal, and your ability to apply these twelve laws. Once you recognize the truth of this matter, you will be free from the gripping fear of losing a job or applying for promotions. You will also cease being emotionally dependent on your employer or on a particular position. You will experience a freedom from fear and a release from whatever binds you to an underemployment condition.

Establishing your career goal, developing a consistently positive attitude, obtaining the right workplace skills, and having faith in God and yourself will sustain you through the tough times and ultimately propel you into career success. You can begin now to face your next career step or promotion acquisition with confidence. You obviously have the personal motivation to excel at the workplace, or you would not have read this entire book in the first place. You can also have confidence in the fact that you have read the right book, know the universal secrets to becoming as indispensable as possible, and now have the opportunity to put your knowledge to work for you. You have the right stuff.

Best wishes!
Tony Zeiss

EPILOGUE

By Ron and Katherine Harper
Harper Companies International

Over a span of forty-six years in the business world, we have read literally hundreds of self help and inspirational books. During all that time we've found that generally two out of ten, or about twenty percent, really grab your attention and offer new and different ideas for achieving success.

This book, The Twelve Essential Laws for Becoming Indispensable, is certainly in that top twenty percent category—in fact, we would place it in the top ten of all the "success" books we have ever read. The amazing part of Dr. Zeiss' advice is that he gives you very practical, clear and readily attainable methods to enable you to become virtually indispensable.

It is our hope that you received the insights and illumination to seek and achieve your greatest career dreams. All the tools for success are in this book and we encourage you to keep it for easy reference when that next promotion opportunity presents itself. Remember to keep a positive attitude, keep learning new employment skills, and stay focused on your customers. With the knowledge presented in this book and just a little effort on your part, you will realize your career dreams and become or remain contented at the workplace!

Appendix A

Characteristics, Skills, and Behaviors Most Valued by Employers

While conducting the research for this book, I asked each of the contributing business executives to list those characteristics, skills, and behaviors that they most valued in employees. I received over thirty different categorical preferences and close to 180 different responses. The following list demonstrates those characteristics, skills, and behaviors these employers most value:

- Positive
- Attitude
- Enthusiasm
- Integrity
- Trustworthiness
- Interpersonal Communication Skills
- Self Motivated
- Ambitious
- Loyal
- Committed to Company
- Knowledge and Skills
- Flexible
- Open Minded
- Willing to Change
- Team Player
- Gets Along With Others
- Goal Oriented
- Focused
- Dependable
- Perseveres
- Compassionate
- Fair
- Teachable
- Creative

Appendix B

Task-Team Analysis
Check sentences that best describe your preferences.
When working, I like to.

___ 1. Complete job assignments on time.

___ 2. Lead a team of coworkers.

___ 3. Produce quality work on my own.

___ 4. Participate in group assignments.

___ 5. Manage my time efficiently.

___ 6. Give directions.

___ 7. Achieve group consensus.

___ 8. Conceive, develop, and implement my ideas.

___ 9. Make sure the job is done with precision.

___10. See others do well at their jobs.

___11. Be part of a team.

___12. Brainstorm with others to reach solutions.

Add all checks for sentences numbered 1, 3, 5, 6, 8,
9. This is your "Task" score. Add all checks for sen-

tences numbered 2, 4, 7, 10, 11, 12. This is your "Team" score.

Employers most appreciate employees who have both high "Task" and high "Team" scores. If you have three or fewer checked sentences in either the "Task" or the "Team" category, you should concentrate on improving your respective low "Task" or "Team" orientation. Employers most desire a proper balance between the two categories.

Appendix C

- **Career Assessment Process**

To determine your basic interests and values, do the following exercises in private. (There are no right or wrong answers.)

Interests

List those activities and hobbies that make you the happiest:

_____

_____

_____

_____

List the names of persons whom you most admire:

_____.

_____.

_____.

Values

Briefly describe what you most admire about each person listed:

_____.

_____.

Now review the exercises and circle the things that most interest you and that you most value. These circled items represent your highest interests and values. As you begin to focus on a job group, keep these interests and values in mind. By choosing a career that features these same attributes, you will definitely be happier and more productive at work.

List six personal accomplishments achieved alone or with a group (they can be things you're proud of from your childhood to today):

1. _____.

2. _____.

3. _____.

4. _____.

5. _____.

6. _____.

Now review these accomplishments and identify the particular part of each accomplishment that you most enjoyed. Was it because you achieved a goal by yourself, because you helped others, or because you exhibited leadership skills? This self-review should also reveal some of your true interests and values.

What is it that you really want to do with your life? This fundamental question needs to be answered before you settle on a career goal because the major part of your life will be spent at the workplace. If you are not happy at your job, you will never excel at it and you will have wasted a good portion of your life. These next exercises are designed to help you focus on your career goal. As you complete these exercises, remember that now is the time of truth. You are doing this for yourself only, and there are no wrong answers.

Pretend that your life ends this very moment. Now list five adjectives your friends would most likely use to describe your personality:

He (or she) was   1. _____

                    2. _____

                    3. _____

                    4. _____

Next, list the five accomplishments your obituary would likely report:

He (or she)   1. _____

                    2. _____

                    3. _____

                    4._____

Now, review your responses. These exercises are intended to help you step away from yourself for a moment and concentrate on who you are and what you have accomplished to this point in your life. If you are unhappy with who you have been and what you have accomplished, you can set higher goals to accomplish. Go back to the exercises, print in bold letters the different or additional adjectives you would like to describe you. In the following spaces, write the job objective or career goal that you would like to accomplish in your lifetime.

Job objective: Within ___ weeks, I will be promoted
_____.

Career goal: I intend to_____
_____.

These descriptors and life goals should become your primary tools for selecting the immediate job objective and long-term career goal. Of course, the simple task of writing these desires on paper is a far cry from achieving them. Behavioral research indicates that you will become and accomplish what you most desire and believe. Therefore, no matter how strange, bold, or different your new pursuits are, you will be successful if you truly want them, believe you can achieve them, and have a good plan to follow.

Appendix D

Career Goal Exercise

The following exercise is the most important in the entire book. Your responses to these five statements will form the core of your career plan and will prepare you with the confidence that comes from knowing yourself and what you can do for an employer. Use only one sentence for each statement.

1. State your immediate job objective.

_____

_____

2. State your career goal (or where you intend to be ten years from now).

_____

_____

3. State why the employer should promote or hire you (specify personality traits).

_____

_____

4. State your specific credentials for the position.

_____

_____

5. State why you've chosen this career field.

_____

_____

The completion of this exercise will result in a five-sentence biography that you can relate in clear language while networking, talking to supervisors, filling out a job application, or responding to an interviewer. You could even have this snappy biography printed on your business cards or on the flap of your personalized thank-you notes!

Appendix E

Academic-Technical Skills Assessment

Complete the following exercises to determine your strengths and weaknesses in the knowledge area.

List all major education and training learned through an educational institution:

High School

_____

_____

_____

College

_____

_____

_____

Military

_____

_____

_____

List all major education and training learned through a job, through a hobby, or through volunteer service:

On-the-Job Training

_____

_____

_____

Hobby or Volunteer Service

_____

_____

_____

Now match your career goals or immediate job objective knowledge and skills requirements to your knowledge and skills listed in this assessment activity. Correct any apparent deficiencies.

Appendix F

Discover Your Personality Traits

Most likely, you easily listed academic subject areas in the Appendix E exercises but found it more difficult to list what you have learned on the job and through hobbies or volunteer service. The purpose of this exercise is to help you realize that subject areas by themselves are not very meaningful to you in the job search process. You and the potential employer need to understand your knowledge base in terms of workplace needs. The following list of social and workplace skills will help to identify your special knowledge or skills in this regard.

Circle the words that best describe your abilities:

Writing	Organizing
Speaking	Arbitrating
Persuading	Motivating
Selling	Conceptualizing
Problem Solving	Detail Oriented
Leading	Socially Sensitive
Creating	Politically Astute
Analyzing	Honest
Managing	Diligent
Coaching	Patient
Cheering	Reliable
Goals Setting	Task Completing
Enthusiastic	Loyal

Once you have completed this exercise, practice describing yourself with the words you have circled. Employers understand these words, and when that important promotion opportunity arrives, you'll be talking their language! To describe yourself as "holding a bachelor's degree in business" is one thing. It's much more meaningful to the employer, however, if you describe yourself as "a creative, loyal, and energetic professional with a degree in business."

About the Author

Tony Zeiss holds a doctorate in higher education and is a nationally recognized leader in workforce development. His thirty years of experience in higher education have been highlighted by his prominence in economic and workforce development.

He supervised the development of one of the first U.S. Department of Labor approved skills centers, chaired the Colorado State Job Training Coordinating Council, and led two colleges into national prominence through his focus on America's workforce. He currently serves as a member of Vice President Gore's Leadership Group For Life Long Learning and is Chairman of the Board for the American Association of Community Colleges.

He is a prolific writer and speaker whose previous books include *Economic Development: a Viewpoint of Business, Creating a Literate Society* (with a preface by Barbara Bush), *Community College Leadership in the Twenty-First Century, The Twelve Essential Laws For Getting A Job,* and *Developing America's Best Work Force.* He is also a popular consultant, a professional speaker, and a boardmember for the Zig Ziglar Corporation.

Dr. Zeiss is currently president of Central Piedmont Community College, which serves 70,000 students each year in Charlotte, North Carolina.